W9-ADE-471

An Experiential
Approach to Group Work

Advisory Editor

Thomas M. Meenaghan, *New York University*

Related books of interest

Interviewing for the Helping Professions: A Relational Approach

Fred R. McKenzie

Social Work Practice with Families: A Resiliency-Based Approach, Second Edition

Mary Patricia Van Hook

Navigating Human Service Organizations, Third Edition

Rich Furman and Margaret Gibelman

Advocacy Practice for Social Justice, Second Edition

Richard Hoefer

Social Work Practice with Latinos: Key Issues and Emerging Themes

Rich Furman and Nalini Negi

Empowering Workers and Clients for Organizational Change

Marcia B. Cohen and Cheryl A. Hyde

Best Practices in Community Mental Health: A Pocket Guide

Vikki L. Vandiver

Getting Your MSW: How to Survive and Thrive in a Social Work Program, Second Edition

Karen M. Sowers and Bruce A. Thyer

An Experiential Approach to Group Work

Second Edition

Rich Furman
University of Washington, Tacoma

Kimberly Bender
University of Denver

Diana Rowan
University of North Carolina, Charlotte

LYCEUM
BOOKS, INC.

Chicago, Illinois

© Lyceum Books, Inc., 2014

Published by

LYCEUM BOOKS, INC.
5758 S. Blackstone Ave.
Chicago, Illinois 60637
773+643-1903 (Fax)
773+643-1902 (Phone)
lyceum@lyceumbooks.com
http://www.lyceumbooks.com

All rights reserved under International and Pan-American Copyright Conventions.
No part of the publication may be reproduced, stored in a retrieval system, copied, or
transmitted in any form or by any means without written permission from the publisher.

6 5 4 3 2   14 15 16

ISBN 978-1-935871-33-0

Library of Congress Cataloging-in-Publication Data

Library of Congress
CIP 20540-4320
9140 East Hampton Drive
Capital Heights, MD 20743

To Slick (1998–2013)

Living with and loving your indomitable spirit inspired me, in more ways than anyone could ever know.

Contents

Preface to the Second Edition

This second edition of *An Experiential Approach to Group Work* provides a significant increase in theory regarding key aspects of group dynamics and process. Readers who enjoyed the practical and experiential approach that we adopted in the first edition should fear not; the fundamental character of the content remains the same. We provide this expanded discussion of theoretical issues (largely confined to the first chapter) in response to classroom instructors who appreciated the first edition but need a resource with more theory to use as their primary text. As textbooks become increasingly expensive, and as social work and related fields continue to teach first generation college students, fiscal considerations are important. Clearly, if we are to speak of social justice, classroom instructors would be wise to consider the cost of the materials we use. This new edition affords instructors the opportunity to assign one textbook, supplemented with articles or other readings to suit specific needs.

In addition, and perhaps more important, we believe that the first edition did not sufficiently contextualize the experiential aspects of group practice with a clear discussion of the theory of group processes and dynamics. As Kurt Lewin, one of the most important group theorists, wrote, "There is nothing so practical as a good theory" (1951, 169). As such, we maintain our experiential, hands-on approach but seek to integrate important classical and modern theories more fully early on in the book.

As we were writing the expanded discussion of group theory, we became a bit worried that classical theories might seem less than relevant to some readers. Thus we also present some modern discussions of the theory of group dynamics, including an exciting approach with a social justice orientation. In keeping with the original, practical nature of the book, we also attempt to help readers clearly understand what to do with this information. Instructors should note, however, that a survey text such as this, covering diverse theoretical ground, cannot escape presenting conflicting ideas and information. In fact, throughout social work education and related disciplines, students will encounter many conflicting theories. Instructors should be prepared to help students understand how to evaluate and integrate diverse ideas.

In this edition we also include materials relevant to Canadian, British, and Australian social work and human service students, faculty, and professionals. We believe that these changes will benefit not only international readers but U.S. readers as well. U.S. social workers and human service practitioners and students are too infrequently afforded opportunities to explore the ideas, scholarship, and professional insights of those from other countries, Canada in particular. This is lamentable, as Canadian scholarship in social work and other helping professions has a distinct flavor and often reflects anti-oppressive models and theories that are neglected in the United States, with our recent privileging of evidence-based practice and the medical model. U.S. readers may find these new perspectives and insights valuable; Canadian readers should find this text more congruent with their pedagogical and practice needs. We also include information from other countries, notably Great Britain, Brazil, Israel, and Colombia, thereby offering more diverse views on the nature of group practice.

Toward this aim, we present three new chapters. We are particularly happy to include chapters 12 and 13 on macro group practice and anti-oppressive group practice. Anti-oppressive perspectives are influential in Canada, Australia, and several countries of Europe. We believe that social work practice in the United States would be well served by paying closer attention to these approaches. The Association for the Advancement of Social Work with Groups (2010) named social justice as one of its two core values of group work practice (along with respect for persons and their autonomy); ethical group work practice should therefore be conducted with such issues in mind.

Chapter 18, the third new chapter, focuses on group work with immigrant populations. As globalization and transnationalism become increasingly influential, social workers will find themselves working with immigrant groups more frequently. Not only will practitioners need to work with these populations locally, but they will also need to consider the transnational nature of immigrants' lives. Over the next decade, social workers will likely take more significant advantage of Internet, telephone, and video technologies to begin practicing transnationally (Furman, Negi, Schatz, and Jones, 2008). For example, a group worker counseling Mexican immigrants living in the United States may find it beneficial to include people from the group members' home communities in Mexico using Internet-based video. Some of you may in fact already be using some of these technologies. If you are not, brace yourself.

With these expansions and additions, our intent is to provide an even more valuable tool in the pursuit of teaching, learning, and practicing group work. We hope you enjoy this new edition.

Preface to the First Edition

This book is about developing group work skills. It is different from many group work books in its emphasis on practical skill building and its focus on experiential learning. Experience has taught us that to become a group leader, you need to lead groups. Merely learning the theoretical rationale for group leadership or coming to understand how one should behave is not nearly enough. Students must be helped to develop a complex set of behaviors that facilitate change within the group context. Written this simply, this may seem obvious. However, many social work programs do not adequately prepare students for practice with groups, because they do not provide them with the context to master group skills. It is often assumed, it seems, that faculty can teach students theory and place them into a group setting for a few weeks, and somehow they will learn how to lead groups. Experience has also taught us that teachers must deconstruct each specific skill and help social work students practice these skills in vivo. Hoping students will be able to bridge the gap between practice and theory in the field leaves too much to chance. In this book, students and practitioners will find dozens of exercises that build practice-tested skills related to important aspects of group work practice. You will learn to modify your skills for practice with different groups of clients in diverse practice settings. A benefit of this experiential, skill-based approach is that it is congruent with the competency-based approach to social work education, which will become the standard for accreditation over the next several years.

There are several important reasons why those who seek to learn group practice must have a good deal of experience practicing the skills of group leadership. First, while many people have years of experience being helpers in one-on-one situations, few have such opportunities that group leaders have. In our everyday lives, we are called upon to help friends, colleagues, and others. Helping others in one-on-one situations is natural and almost routine. Such is not the case with our group experiences. While we all have experience being members of groups, rarely do we learn to be change agents in groups. We need to learn what skills are required to facilitate change within groups, and to practice these skills. Second, what might constitute good helping behaviors in one-on-one dyadic situations differs from what is effective in groups. Third, most social work field experiences emphasize individual and family work rather than group work; educational programs must help students gain mastery of group skills. Fourth, group work is a wonderful means of bridging the too often artificial divide between micro and macro practice.

At the beginning of each chapter, we briefly explore the most salient concepts taken from empirical research and theoretical writings related to the subject of the chapter. This is followed by experiential exercises, reflective exercises, case studies, and other exercises, each of which is designed to help new and experienced group workers expand and deepen what they already know. The chapters help build upon your existing strengths, reframing generalist and advanced skills toward effective group work practice.

This book is designed for both foundation and advanced courses in group work, as well as those courses that have or need significant group work content. It is organized into three parts. The first part addresses each of the stages of group practice. We find that helping students sequentially practice the skills associated with each stage of group development allows them to more fully learn each skill. In this part, we have a chapter dedicated specifically to group evaluation, a feature not found in some group work books. Throughout each chapter you will note a focus on developing the capacity for self-reflection and the professional use of self. Of particular note is our focus on the psychosocial and emotional aspects to ending individual group sessions and terminating groups. The second part consists of chapters that explore the major types of groups. We begin with an in-depth discussion of the skills that apply to all groups and then discuss the refinement of these skills as they apply to support (mutual aid), treatment, psychoeducational, and task groups. The last part provides examples of group work practice with some important special populations. In this part, as in others, you will find case examples that bring to life the practice skills we explore. You will develop an understanding of how culturally competent practice can be applied with these populations.

Each chapter begins with a brief discussion of the skills that you will learn from that chapter. These discussions provide the intellectual foundation for your experiential work. At times, we will discuss important findings from research; at other times, we will explore theoretical or ethical concerns. In each chapter, we shall briefly highlight some of the important practice considerations of which you need to be aware. Each provides different types of guidance for group work situations. Following each introduction, you will find exercises that are designed to build your skills in relation to the topic, problem, or population that is presented. In each chapter, you will find exercises that you can do by yourself and exercises to be conducted in class. These exercises will be an important part of your development of group skills, as increased practice will lead to increased mastery. Finally, you will also find exercises that you can use as you lead your own groups. Please share these with your colleagues, and feel free to adapt them to the needs and demands of your agency and group context.

The exercises in this book have been classroom tested. They have been honed over the course of twenty years of combined teaching experience in human service, BSW, and MSW programs. They are based upon our experience as group work practitioners with children with mental health disorders, adults with HIV/AIDS, Latinos suffering from substance abuse, and many other practice contexts.

The exercises are also based upon our recognition that regardless of the theoretical orientation that a social worker holds, the use of self and self-awareness is an essential practice skill. You will find many opportunities in this book for self-reflection through writing exercises, classroom discussion, and critical reflection upon lived practice experience. You will be guided through exercises and asked to reflect upon your own practice, which will help you integrate new skills into your behavioral repertoire. You will also have the opportunity to develop your own philosophy and theoretical framework for group practice.

Following the introduction to the tradition of groups in social work provided in chapter 1, chapter 2 addresses issues around planning a group. Too often, group leaders neglect this all-too-important part of the life of a group. Workers who spend time planning their groups feel better prepared than those who do not. Ironically, the more planning the worker does for his or her group, the more he or she may be free to let go of those plans and act with spontaneity when that is called for (Kurland, 1978).

Chapter 3 explores how to begin a group. The primary purpose of the beginning stage of group is group formation. The early sessions of group life can be very stressful for workers and clients alike. As clients adapt to the nature of the group, they begin to find ways of investing in the group versus maintaining their autonomy. In this chapter, you will learn how important it is for group leaders to explore their own perceptions around what groups are, and you will engage in exercises and experiences that will help you learn some of the key skills for starting a group.

Chapter 4 focuses on the working stage of the group. In this chapter, we continue the exploration of group dynamics and processes that were discussed in the previous chapter. We also explore the importance of group leadership. Even in groups in which the group worker sees himself or herself as more of a facilitator, the manner in which the group worker leads is important.

In chapter 5, we address the importance of group workers evaluating their own behaviors in group and the outcomes of clients. As evidence-based practice and other research-based models become more influential in social work practice, social workers will increasingly be called upon to assess their interventions. Practice evaluation is particularly important in group practice, where the worker must attend to many complex processes. By consciously and systematically building evaluation into your practice, you will become more responsible for client outcomes.

Chapter 6 concludes this part of the book with an exploration of endings. Whether it is the end of a session or the entire group, endings are difficult for many group leaders. In this part, we explore the reasons why this is so and present concrete suggestions and exercises to help workers develop the skills they need to navigate endings.

In the next five chapters, you will learn the differences between some of the key types of social work groups, and information on how they work. You will also engage in exercises that will help you learn how to lead these groups.

While the whole book is focused on helping you develop the skills and competencies that you will need for group practice, in chapter 7, we explore some of the key skills that you will need to develop as a group leader. It will set the context for subsequent chapters. It is helpful to think of the skills that you learn as tools for a metaphorical toolbox, a toolbox that will teach you to apply core competencies to unique and novel practice contexts.

In chapter 8, we address support groups, which also are called mutual aid groups. These groups have an especially important place in social work practice. Shulman (2006) believes that the mutual aid aspect of group life lies at the heart of the utility of group work for the profession. In this chapter, we explore the importance of empathy and problem solving. We look at the nature of the leader's role, which is to remove barriers to mutual support. We also discuss the nature of the client's role, which must be carefully deconstructed for clients in order for the mutual aid groups to be successful.

Chapter 9 explores treatment or clinical groups. As the profession of social work has moved increasingly toward evidence-based practice, clinical services have become ever more important. This chapter presents research on treatment groups and helps workers develop some of the requisite skills for leading these groups.

Chapter 10 explores the value and importance of psychoeducational groups. Psychoeducational groups are important in a variety of settings and demand that social workers develop a different set of skills from what they use in other types of group settings. In psychoeducational groups, the worker must learn to be an effective teacher so group members can integrate new knowledge for improving their thinking, feeling, and behavior.

In chapter 11, we explore task groups. Task groups are an essential part of organizational life in all social service agencies. When run effectively, task groups are a wonderful means of pooling collective wisdom, energy, and skills in service of the completion of key organizational aims. When done poorly, task groups can be a source of endless frustration and can do a good deal of harm to an organization's culture. In this chapter, we explore some of the important tools and skills needed to conduct and participate in successful task groups.

Following chapter 11, we move from the discussion of different types of groups to examples of group work with different populations. Group work has been allied to work with many populations; it is beyond the scope of any introductory book to discuss work with all populations. As such, we have relied on our expertise and practice experiences to present you with chapters that illustrate group work with six different populations.

Eating disorders are an increasingly common type of psychological disorder that social workers need to address. Anorexia and bulimia are not only psychological disorders, but problems with strong social causes and effects. Social norms around body image and gender have strong implications for group workers who are called to work with those suffering from these ailments. Chapter 14 presents guidance on the types of groups that have been shown to be effective with persons suffering from eating disorders.

One of the contexts in which group work has maintained a central place is in the provision of services to persistently mentally ill adults. Community mental health centers have long used psychoeducational and support groups in working with persons suffering from severe and persistent mental illnesses. Chapter 15 demonstrates the scope of group work with this vulnerable population.

In chapter 16, we explore a highly specialized group: conflict resolution groups within elementary schools. With the increase in highly publicized incidences of school violence over the last several years, creating safe and nonviolent school contexts is extremely important. However, as schools contend with increased demands and expectations to provide more with less, fewer nonacademic personnel may be available to provide direct services. As such, we anticipate the role of these groups to take on increased importance over the next several years.

Other important and highly specialized groups are those designed to provide services to pregnant teens. Pregnant teens, who often feel isolated and alone, can receive a great deal of mutual support and acceptance and practice skills in groups. Chapter 17 addresses the complex developmental and social needs of these young women.

Latinos are now the largest minority population in the United States. A diverse population, Latinos are expected to constitute nearly a quarter of the population of the United States within the next several decades. In chapter 19, we explore how groups can be valuable in work with Latino clients. Social workers who have linguistic and cultural competence to work with Latinos will find themselves in high demand.

Chapter 20 explores group work practice with HIV-positive clients and clients with AIDS. While HIV/AIDS has received less attention in the popular media over the last decade, within some communities, its prevalence is rising.

Acknowledgments

I would like to first thank my fine colleagues, Kim and Diana—two wonderful social workers, scholars, teachers, and people—for their wonderful contributions to this book. I am grateful for the skills and passion they brought to this project. From the moment we began discussing our work for this book, I knew that I was in good hands. I would also like to thank my children, Myah and Rebecca, and hope someday they will read and appreciate this book and know that their love is the true ink on its pages. To my wife, Jill, my partner on this wacky ride through time, I am grateful for your love and support. To Brownie, who rested on my lap and helped me endure the hours of writing with his comfort. Lastly, to Bonker—thanks for being my "big fuzzy" during your retirement months. We wish you could have stayed longer, but we feel grateful to have had you in our lives.

Rich Furman

As this project has progressed, I've gained awareness of the many miraculous groups of which I am a member. My sincere thanks to my writing group, Rich and Diana—you made this experience a pleasure. Deep gratitude to my family, who instilled in me the importance of social work practice. And finally, a special thanks to my support group, Matthew Gildner and Nalini Negi, among others, who always encourage me to push on and take deserved rests.

Kimberly Bender

I wish to acknowledge my patients in the adult chemical dependency unit at Charter Real Hospital. You were my first teachers of the symbiotic nature of group work. And to all my private practice group clients, thanks for sharing. This author wishes to disclose that early drafts of this book were written during long evenings and nights spent under a mosquito net in Malawi during a research trip.

Diana Rowan

Chapter 1

The Group Work Tradition in Social Work

> Social group work is a very positive and optimistic way of working with people. It is truly empowering and affirming of people's strengths. In fact, the very act of forming a group is a statement of belief in people's strengths and in the contribution that each person can make in the others' lives. (Kurland & Salmon, 1998, p. ix)

Magical things happen within groups. Ask any experienced group worker, and he or she will have numerous stories about how groups have changed the lives of his or her clients. Indeed, research has demonstrated group work to be effective with many types of problems, including substance abuse (Humphreys, 1999), compulsive disorders (Ladouceur, Sylvain, Boutin, Lachance, Doucet, & Leblond, 2003), mental illness (Spidel, Lecomte, & Leclerc, 2006), posttraumatic stress disorder (Mueser, Bolton, Carty, Bradley, Ahlgren, DiStaso, et al., 2007), and Alzheimer's and other forms of dementia (Bank, Arguelles, Rubert, Eisdorfer, & Czaja, 2006). In times of scarce resources, group work may be a particularly important approach, as workers can effectively serve many clients at the same time. By using groups, social workers can often negotiate the frequent tension between cost containment and service provision.

Work with various populations is central to the mission of the profession of social work (National Association of Social Workers, 2000). Group work is one of the most important methods of culturally sensitive practice (Salvendy, 1999; Weinberg, 2003). Some of the various populations with which groups have been effectively used are older adults (Tadaka & Kanagawa, 2007), veterans, African Americans (Washington & Moxley, 2003), and Latinos (Díaz, Fuenmayor, & Piedrahita, 2007; Organista, 2000). Groups are an important approach for work with many at-risk and vulnerable populations (Ephross, 2005) and have been shown to be useful in both long-term (Gitterman & Shulman, 2005) and short-term treatment (Rosenbaum, 1996; Shapiro, Peltz, & Bernadett-Shapiro, 1998; Wing Lo, 2005).

Like many other institutions and social structures, social work has been greatly affected by globalization (Furman & Negi, 2007) and has been increasingly internationalized. As many cultures of the world are far more collectivist (group and communally oriented) than we are in the United States (which is far more individualistic), group work is an appropriate method for international practice. For example, clinical groups are used for working with the poor in Singapore (Devan, 2001), and community empowerment groups have been an important intervention in organizing poor disempowered laborers throughout Latin America.

In this chapter, we will briefly explore this history and present a beginning discussion of the key concepts of group work. At this point, and we shall stress this at many times in this and other chapters, your ability to be an effective group worker will depend upon your ability to reflect upon your practice and put these reflections into action. The notion of the reflective practitioner is not new and has been viewed as essential in social work for decades (Schön, 1983). Throughout this book, you will be asked to reflect upon the information that is presented to you and engage in exercises and experiences that will help you take ownership of group work skills. We hope you will learn these skills so well that over time you will be able to adapt them to new situations in novel ways. While this type of integration has been discussed by many authors in social work (Furman, 2007; Ringel, 2003), it was perhaps most fully explored by Brazilian educator Paolo Freire. Freire (1970) explores how through reflection and practice, theory is integrated into the behavioral repertoire of the practitioner; new theory and skill are generated through continued exploration of each of these domains.

Group work makes sense for social work, as human beings spend a good deal of their lives living, working, and loving in the context of groups. Social work is the profession that focuses on the person within the context of his or her environment. That is, social work not only helps individuals adapt to their environments but also helps environments adapt to the needs, dreams, goals, and aspirations of individuals. It is this person-in-environment orientation that makes groups especially valuable as a tool of social work practice. Think of the group as a microcosm of society, and group work as an opportunity to help individuals improve their social relationships and resources through their interactions in the group. Imagine a group as a potential catalyst for social change, in which individuals come together to develop effective strategies for changing their external social worlds. Alternatively, envision a group as a place where people suffering from a serious disease can come together for support, acceptance, and hope. These are some of the many potential uses for groups that we will explore in this book.

What Is a Group?

Throughout the years, social workers and other helping professionals have developed different definitions and conceptualizations of groups. A consideration of these definitions is important, as each can lead practitioners to focus on different aspects of group practice. For our purposes, when we refer to a group, we are referring to a social work practice group. In sociology, political science, and common everyday language, the term *group* has different meanings than it does for social work practice. In those contexts, the word *group* often refers to an eth-nic group or a large number of people who have similar historical and cultural experiences.

Schwartz (1971) provides a simple definition when he notes that a social work group is "a collection of people who need each other in order to work on cer-tain common tasks, in an agency hospitable to those tasks" (p. 7). Anderson (1997) observes that social work practice with groups is a methodology for the empowerment of group members to improve the quality of their lives. The focus is on members' growth. The intent is to stimulate their autonomous growth process through participation in a group process. Shulman (2009) views the group as an enterprise in mutual aid, an alliance of individuals who need each other, in varying degrees, to work on certain common problems. He refers to the group as a "mutual aid system."

The History of Group Work

While the tradition of group work in the profession is rich, it is also one marked by conflict and ambivalence. Before the start of social work as a profession, ser-vices were provided by various community-based and faith-based individuals and groups. At the turn of the twentieth century, group workers and case-workers often experienced tense relationships. A great deal of misunderstand-ing existed concerning their roles, and about group work in particular. This ten-sion in the profession continues to exist to this day between those who advocate social change and transformation and those who view the profession more in terms of individual change and the medical model. Individual caseworkers, whose beliefs stemmed from the moral model of treatment (Jackson, 2001), focused on the responsibilities of the individual and his or her character in the helping relationship. Early group workers were more likely to view social condi-tions, such as the Industrial Revolution, urbanization, or the unequal distribution of wealth, as the cause of social problems. As such, early group workers were focused on social change, while individual caseworkers tended to see pathology as resting within the individual.

Early group workers were less likely to be limited to the use of what were seen as high-status activities, such as therapy; they therefore exhibited a great deal of creativity and borrowed methods from the arts and humanities. These workers were more likely to use means involving action and participation, such as recre-ation groups, the arts, and community mobilization, as methods of intervention. Workers who wanted the social work profession to be viewed as an influential and high-status profession often viewed these activities as recreation, not pro-fessional in nature. These methods became less popular over time, as social workers began to view these adjunctive methods as resting outside the realm of professional practice.

The end of World War II marked an important time in the development of clinical group methods. Psychiatrists, overwhelmed by the number of returning veterans with psychological problems, began seeing veterans in pairs or groups, not for therapeutic reasons but out of necessity. Also, with the introduction of early psychotropic medication, the profession increasingly began to view the individual as the focus of practice.

In the 1950s, the professional society that was concerned with group work joined with other societies to create the National Association of Social Work. This affiliation unified the many different methods of the profession into one organization. Over the next twenty years, many schools of social work introduced group work concentrations, in which students focused on group work in the second year of their MSW program.

In the 1960s, group work in social work and other helping professions was used increasingly as a vehicle for social change. Consciousness-raising groups and groups used in War on Poverty programs helped empower women and ethnic minorities to fight alienation and seek control over their communities. Groups (sit-ins) were used as a tool of education during protests against the Vietnam War, and by activists in the civil rights movement. This energy and creativity was reflected in the teaching of group skills in social work education programs.

Over the last two decades, however, the role of groups within social work education has declined. Few programs offer concentrations, and many do not even offer a course dedicated solely to group work. The diminution of group work in social work education and practice is unfortunate for several reasons. First, group work is not viewed as a significant part of social work history. Second, numerous studies have demonstrated the efficacy of group work in many types of social work practice. Third, group work encourages the type of social relationships and collective empowerment that are congruent with social work values and ethics. Fourth, group work (in the form of task groups such as staff meetings and committees) is a ubiquitous aspect of the organizational life of social agencies; good group work is essential to the functioning of the profession.

Still, group work remains an important part of the practice of many social workers. Social workers must possess good group work skills for work with groups in micro and macro practice.

Practice Contexts

Social workers are called on to run groups in all settings. When one considers the prevalence of task groups (to be discussed later in this chapter) in administrative life and case conference groups in which clients are discussed, it is hard to imagine a social worker who is not or will not be part of groups frequently. Social workers are called upon to run groups at the micro and the macro levels. Social workers work in groups as therapists, advocates, organizers, leaders, brokers, facilitators, and collaborators. In the next section, we will explore the different types of groups that social workers lead. Each of these groups calls for different tasks and actions, based upon the purpose of the group. First, however, we want to address a few of the most common practice contexts and issues that are increasingly shaping the context of group practice.

Managed Care

Since the 1970s, managed care organizations have had a profound influence on social work practice. With their alignment with the medical model and the medical profession, managed care organizations have had a profound impact on social work in general, and social work with groups in particular. Striving for efficacy, managed care organizations have encouraged social workers to focus on problems that are measurable and can be resolved in a limited number of sessions. As such, managed care organizations have contributed to groups moving away from more community-based and empowerment models, and toward clinical groups designed to ameliorate symptoms. As such, some of the types of groups that will be explored will be less familiar to social workers today than to those in the past.

Globalization and Diversity

The Latino population is now the largest ethnic minority group in the United States. Areas that traditionally have been mostly white, or perhaps white and African American, have seen increases in the Latino and Asian American communities. Emigration resulting from genocide and famine in Africa has significantly increased the African populations throughout the United States. As social workers are increasingly called upon to serve these different cultural populations, group workers must develop culturally competent group work skills. Throughout this book, we will provide case examples from several populations and explore many issues that are important to consider in working with various communities.

Not only do social workers face increasingly diverse communities in the United States, but as the world becomes more globalized, social workers will work with various populations in new ways. As various populations become increasingly transnational in nature—that is, as they more frequently move across boundaries and nations—social work will need to become transnational as well. Group workers in the future will be called upon to use Internet-based technologies, such as video conferencing and inexpensive telephonic communications, to facilitate group processes for individuals living in different countries. For instance, migrant rights groups here and in Mexico could be helped to work together through these technologies.

Types of Groups

Social workers lead many types of groups. Agencies may refer to groups by different names (e.g., a staff meeting is a type of task group, or a therapy group may be called a counseling group); thus, if you are unclear about the nature of the group you are going to run, ask for clarification. While groups certainly can be hybrids of different kinds of groups, the purpose of a group is one of the most important factors that determine how successful it will be. Be innovative and creative, but always with clear aims and goals in mind.

Educational Groups

The purpose of educational groups is for group members to learn specific information. In educational groups, the focus is not on the group members' feelings or behavior, but on their acquisition of new knowledge. For example, a social worker in a job training program may lead an educational group on how to fill out job applications or how to select references.

Therapy Groups

Therapy groups, or counseling groups, seek to help members explore their feelings, thoughts, and behaviors for the purpose of lasting change. Therapy groups can be either short term or long term and often focus on a particular problem, such as depression, anxiety disorders, or the effects of child abuse. Cognitive-behavioral therapy groups are one of the most popular types of therapy groups, and there is a great deal of evidence to support their efficacy.

Psychoeducational Groups

While in educational groups the focus is on the material to be learned, and in therapy the focus is on personal growth and change, psychoeducational groups have a dual focus. The purpose of psychoeducational groups is to use information and educational processes to facilitate individual growth.

Task Groups

Social workers who claim that they do not do group work because they are not direct practitioners forget how much administrative work is actually done in groups. Task groups, which are groups in which specific work functions are accomplished, are ubiquitous parts of agency life. Staff meetings, committee meetings, groups designed to work on agency policies and procedures, and many community meetings have the purpose of meeting predetermined work goals.

Support Groups

Support groups differ from therapy groups in that the goal of the group is not personality change or helping people recover from a problem such as mental illness or substance abuse. The premise of support groups is that when healthy human beings encounter difficult life situations, they can benefit from support, caring, and mutual aid. An example of a support group is a group for parents who have lost their children to cancer or other diseases.

Self-Help Groups

Self-help groups are those that are not led by helping professionals. Self-help groups, by definition, are led by group participants, usually members who have been involved in the organization for some time. Twelve-step programs are the most popular self-help groups. Twelve-step groups such as Alcoholics Anonymous, Overeaters Anonymous, and Gamblers Anonymous encourage peer support both within and outside the group settings to help members recover from their problems. While social workers are not directly involved in running twelve-step groups, they frequently work with clients who are members of twelve-step programs. Since twelve-step support groups are based upon spiritual/religious principles, they are not appropriate for all social work clients. Social workers should seek out other self-help groups that are not religiously based for those clients who would be uncomfortable with such an approach.

Community Organizing Groups

As community organization has become a less influential method in social work practice and education, community organizing groups have become a less common form of practice. This is lamentable, as groups can be an especially valuable tool for promoting community change. Through groups, community members can share their common concerns and explore impediments to and strategies for change. In one community, a group worker helped community members develop strategies for reducing the amount of crime and violence that they experienced. The group worker helped community members connect with police groups, investigate strategies for neighborhood watches, and organize community graffiti cleanups. Over time, the community became a safer place to live. Alone, residents felt powerless and ineffectual. By coming together in a group, they developed a shared sense of responsibility, hope, and empowerment. Working together, they were able to brainstorm ideas that they would not have come up with on their own.

Empowerment/Liberation Groups

Although less common than they once were in the United States, empowerment and liberation groups remain a popular method of social work practice throughout the developing world. The purpose of empowerment/liberation groups is to help members develop awareness of the source of their own oppression, and to help members empower each other to transcend this oppression. This work has been informed by the writings and practice of Paolo Freire (1970). In using these methods, group leaders guide members to critical reflection on the nature of their life contexts. Reflective questions such as, Why are they poor when others are rich? How are they kept poor? What is the nature of their education, and how does this keep them oppressed? are used. The goal of this empowerment-oriented work is to help people develop personal and political awareness of how their lives have been affected by racism and oppression. Empowerment groups seek to help people take personal and political power, individually and collectively. Throughout Latin America, these groups have been used with the dual purpose of education and empowerment.

Group Dynamics and Processes

For those new to groups, or perhaps better said, for those new to learning about groups, the concepts of group dynamics and group processes are often difficult to understand. There are several reasons for this. First, the manner in which people interact in groups is different than how they act in dyadic, or one-on-one, relationships. Since these are the most common form of day-to-day relationships in most Western societies, most people tend to understand human life through the lens of dyadic relationships. Learning to see the world through the lens of group life is therefore difficult for many people. Second, those with experience working with individuals have learned skills and concepts of helping that often do not apply to groups. Because many of us have worked hard to acquire these skills, it is natural that we rely heavily on them. Third, the very nature of the terms *dynamics* and *processes* are somewhat nebulous. Both terms are typically used interchangeably. Last, different authors have very different views on the nature of these two concepts. In this section, we describe how these different ways of conceptualizing what happens in groups influence practice. Learning these theories will expand your ability to assess what is happening in groups and to plan interventions based on the needs of your specific group.

A key concept of group processes is the distinction between task and maintenance functions. Task functions are the "what" of the group, while maintenance functions refer to how these aims are achieved (Westwood, Mak, Barker, & Ishiyama, 2000). Maintenance, then, is another way of referring to the notion of group process, the notion that there exist factors that one can facilitate to encourage the healthy functioning of a group, outside of the actual content or tasks to be engaged in. In the following discussion of group processes, you will note that these processes can and do occur without intervention; that is, they are part of the naturally occurring processes of the group. However, this does not mean that a group leader is helpless to alter the dynamics and pattern of a group; understanding the naturally occurring processes can help group leaders plan interventions to challenge and support the healthy development of group processes and dynamics.

Underlying all theories, approaches, and definitions of group processes is the notion that people behave differently in groups than they do outside of groups. That is, there is something about the group experience itself that influences how people behave. According to this notion, one cannot understand the behavior of individuals in a group in isolation; an assessment of individuals' personalities, characteristics, and differences is not enough to account for their behavior. Something more must be occurring to explain the ways that individuals interact with, learn from, empower, enrich, and inhibit each other. This "something more" is what is referred to as group dynamics or processes. Group dynamics or processes, which we shall use interchangeably here, are social forces that exert influence on the behavior of individuals within the context of groups. Theories and approaches to group dynamics not only have been useful in social work and human service–oriented groups but also have been important to business and management, team sports, and education.

Group dynamics are so powerful that they often lead people to act in ways that are not easily explained by the attributes of these individuals. Early explorers of group dynamics and sociological forces have observed that people who are not cruel and violent by nature can become so in the context of problematic groups and powerful social forces. For example, cult members at the Jonestown community who were not depressed or suicidal nevertheless killed themselves with poisoned punch, due in large part to the power of group dynamics (Ulman & Abse, 1983).

Just as disturbing, one of the classical early experiments on power and control within prisons, known as the Stanford Prison Experiment, showed just how powerful group persuasion and culture can be (Haney & Zimbardo, 1998). Members of the experiment (college students, not those convicted of crimes) were divided into the roles of prison guards and prisoners, and they performed their roles far more realistically than the experimenters had anticipated. Those in the role of prison guards engaged in considerable psychological abuse, and because of the pressure of group and social forces, other "prisoners" and even the lead researcher neglected to intervene. Although some of these forces do go beyond classical group dynamics, in that it is debatable if the members of the Stanford Prison Experiment formed a group as we consider them in social work and human service practice, what is important to note is how social forces can influence people's behavior as much as their own personal histories, personalities, strengths, and weaknesses can.

For this reason, it is not enough for social workers to merely understand theories of individual development or personality when attempting to understand the behavior of clients in groups. Group dynamics and processes add a layer that makes working in groups fascinating, complex, and at times frustrating to those not trained in group methods.

How then do you use these theories? How do you make them practical? We want you to think of each of these theories as tools to help increase your understanding. We shall stress this point in several ways in this chapter. The theories do not speak of what must happen in groups, but of possibilities. By understanding the nature of what is happening, and understanding that what is occurring is "normal," you can learn to be less reactive and upset, and instead be more calm and thoughtful in selecting ways of intervening (or, in many cases, not intervening!). In this book, you will learn to integrate theory, skills, and values as you practice the many exercises in each section. Rest assured, the more you practice, the more you will begin to own the ideas presented here.

The term *group dynamics* first appeared in the work of Kurt Lewin (1951). Lewin was a Prussian/Jewish scholar whose interest in groups stemmed from his concerns about war and the oppression of others. He was also troubled by Freudian explanations of behavior, which focused on individuals' unresolved intrapsychic conflicts. From his own research, Lewin found that diverse individuals brought together would actually behave in a manner that suggested that the nature of the group experience profoundly influences individual behavior. As such, Lewin took the insights of sociological and anthropological ways of understanding the world and applied them to groups. It was Lewin who brought the study of the group from a study of diverse individuals with their own "stuff" to our current understanding of groups as a system. These insights seem, perhaps, obvious to us now, but they were almost revolutionary at the time.

According to Brown (1988), two of Lewin's insights are particularly applicable to the understanding of group dynamics: interdependence of fate and task interdependence. According to Lewin, group members bond and develop a sense of cohesiveness when they perceive that their fates are tied together. Similarly, when group members perceive that successful completion of tasks and goals is predicated on working well together, they are likely to become more invested in the group. Lewin believed that task interdependence was a stronger force than independence of fate, an important insight for group facilitators.

These two insights, which seem logical and intuitive, form the backbone of many theories of group dynamics and modern group practice. For example, Jacobs, Masson, and Harvill's (2001) system of group work, although therapeutic in nature, relies extensively on the completion of specific group tasks. Similarly, anti-oppressive group work focuses on individuals moving from the development of a shared consciousness about the nature of their oppression to collective, coordinated action. In anti-oppressive and social justice approaches to practice, not only are social change goals fostered through coordinated group action, but the power of healthy group dynamics can help individuals meet many of their psychosocial needs (Hays, Arredondo, Gladding, & Toporek, 2010; Sakamoto & Pitner, 2005).

Shutz (1958) was another important early contributor to our understanding of group process. Shutz posited that groups will function best when group members are compatible in three domains: inclusion, control, and trust. According to Shutz, groups comprising people who have higher levels of compatibility in these three domains will perform their tasks and functions better than those who do not. There are two main implications of this notion. The first is that group leaders should work to form groups that are heterogeneous in nature. The second is that, because heterogeneous groups cannot always be formed given the great diversity of group membership, group leaders should learn to help members navigate their differences. As you read through the next section on stage theories, you will find that the issues of inclusion, control, and trust have made their way into various theories, albeit at times using different terms. This makes sense, as each of these concepts is related to key developmental and relational tasks that each of us encounter throughout our lives.

Stage Theories

In an effort to explain how groups work, theorists have attempted to describe the ways in which group dynamics influence human behavior. One of the most common systems for describing group dynamics are stage theories. Stage theories of group behavior, as with theories of development applied to individuals, seek to describe how groups move through their "life course." As Westwood, Mak, Barker, and Ishiyama (2000) explain, "Stage theory of group development enables leaders to anticipate and predict the type and quality of group interactions to be expected and how the various stages in the group influence learning among the participants" (p. 325). While stage theories can be very helpful, it is important to remember that such theories are guidelines only, and variance does exist.

Tuckman's Classic Model

Tuckman (1965) developed the most well-known model of group stage theories. Tuckman posited that groups move through four stages of development: forming, storming, norming, and performing. Tuckman and Jensen (1977) later updated this theory to include the adjourning stage.

During the forming stage, group members are on their best behavior as they strive to put forth a good presentation and be accepted by other group members. During this stage, group members get to know each other and begin to exchange personal information about themselves. The forming stage is characterized by reliance on the group leader and compliance with the stated goals and objectives of the group. This stage is also characterized by efforts to fit in and be accepted. Several group leadership skills are important during this phase. First, group leaders must be able to develop a safe and accepting climate, whereby members begin to feel comfortable with each other. During this phase, group leaders should learn how to help members identify commonalities within the group.

Tuckman's next stage, storming, is characterized by a heightening of tension within the group, as some of the basic assumptions, rules, and norms are challenged. Tuckman views this as a normal, and in fact necessary, stage of group development. During this phase, the group leader must be able to successfully navigate varying levels of conflicts; being able to resolve these conflicts successfully helps group members feel an increased sense of intimacy and commitment to their work. Within this phase, norms and rules are pushed, but the group leader's enforcement of them provides a container and a structure for positive resolution. Group leaders must develop the capacity to be self-reflective, calm, and nondefensive to successfully manage this stage. As group members may often project blame onto the group leader, group leaders must develop the capacity to manage their emotions and carefully monitor their own reactions. Because of such difficulties during the storming phase, some leaders prefer co-leadership. Having a colleague there to support you and validate the difficulty of such experiences can be invaluable.

In the norming stage, group members learn that they can trust one another. During this phase, they begin to develop a sense of closeness and intimacy. The degree to which this closeness develops depends on the nature of the group. For example, just as most task-oriented and education-oriented groups do not go through nearly as intense storming as some other group types, so too, such groups are not characterized by the same level of intimacy. Yet, even within these groups, trust is an important aspect of the group process, which, according to this theory, actually develops from a successful resolution of group conflict. From this sense of closeness, a group identity is formed that leads to a sense of cohesiveness, through which the possibility of moving toward the work of the group becomes a reality. As clients may be new to groups, group leaders should establish clear guidelines or facilitate the development of clear rules and norms.

In the performing stage, the group settles into the work that it will conduct. The term *work* can refer to a variety of types of change, from interpersonal change, community empowerment, organizational transformation, or the creation of a work product. The ability to perform is predicated, according to this model, on the ability of members to trust each other, to be clear about their roles, and to understand and have bought into the norms of the group. In other words, the group's previous struggles were necessary to set the stage for conducting the work of the group. In this stage, the group leader must be familiar with various theories of change and help engage the group and its members in a problem-solving process.

In the adjourning stage, the group, having completed its work, can disband. This disbanding does not always coincide with the completion of the work for many people, as is the case for therapy and other personal change groups. Social work group practice may at times differ from some other professions during this phase, as social work views the process of case management and the linking of group members to new services as essential tasks. Depending on the nature of the leader's role, some social work group leaders, such as those in community mental health centers or in medical facilities, will continue to work with group members through a case management process.

Although Tuckman's theory has been extremely influential to group work, it has not been without its detractors. For instance, Cassidy (2007) posited that the storming stage may not truly be a necessary phenomenon, and that group leaders expecting to witness this phase may inadvertently contribute to and encourage conflict. Research findings have also suggested that not all groups go through each of the stages, and often not in the same order (Miller, 2003). As with other stage theories, Tuckman's theory may illustrate tendencies, not exact developmental patterns. In spite of some of these concerns, many practitioners have found this theory to be a valuable guide in helping them understand group dynamics. We recommend that you think of each of these stages not as absolute truths but as hypotheses about what may occur in a group. As we have previously noted, by understanding each of these possible stages, you will be increasingly prepared for what may occur. Additionally, you can match the social work skills that you have already developed to the issues at hand. For instance, it is likely that in your first social work practice courses you learned a good deal about helping people deal with conflict, and how to respond with empathy to clients who are resistant or angry. As you move through this book, you will develop many of the skills needed to help groups navigate the terrain of each of the group dynamics explored here, regardless of whether or not they occur in the sequence described.

Anderson's Five-Stage Model

Anderson (1997) presents a five-stage model that highlights the key issues that we discuss throughout this book. In this model, stages correspond to key themes that must be resolved.

Pre-affiliation/trust. The first stage of the group is referred to as pre-affiliation. The people who have come to the group do not yet see themselves as being part of the group. In a very real sense, they are exploring what investment in the group would mean to them, and if they should, on an emotional level, commit themselves as members. The key issue during this phase of group development is trust. As people begin to trust each other and trust the group leader, they come to invest more in the group.

Power and control/autonomy. The second stage of group life involves issues of power and control. Now that members are part of the group, they struggle with making it their own versus being "owned" by the group. In other words, they fight being dominated by the group and seek a sense of autonomy. In this stage, conflict is likely to occur. By working through conflict together, members experience an even greater sense of trust, which brings us to the next phase.

Intimacy/closeness. In human relationships, closeness only occurs in the context of conflict. Knowing that they can disagree with others without the fear of being abandoned enables people to let their guards down and be themselves. This is especially true in the life of a group. A group that successfully negotiates power struggles and the fight for personal autonomy can be a powerful place for the real and honest expression of feelings. In the context of this closeness, group members can take emotional and behavioral risks that they never thought possible.

Differentiation/independence. As a group begins to move toward its ending, members struggle with becoming emotionally separate from the group. This can be painful, as the group comes to represent the venue of many positive changes. It is therefore important that the group leader help members begin to meet their needs outside the group. For instance, a person who has never opened up to others before can begin to do so outside the group. Members can be helped, through case management, to connect to other resources in their communities. The group leader must also help people begin to deal with the emotional pains of separation and abandonment, which must be dealt with in the last phase of the group.

Separation/termination. During the last sessions, group members begin to directly address their feelings of loss and separation. It is often tempting for group workers to rush endings, as they can be painful. Paying attention to the importance of separating well is a key function of group work practice. It is important to remember that good endings are essential in life for good beginnings.

Dimensions of Social Justice Model

Ratts and Santos (2010) present a very different stage model of group work. Their model, termed the Dimensions of Social Justice Model, does not explore the stages that groups *must* or *do* go through, but the stages that they *should* go through. The model assesses what stage a group is at in terms of its social justice orientation. The authors stress that the stages are not only related to or for group members but also should guide group leaders as they plan and execute their groups. The five stages identified by the authors are naïveté, multicultural integration, liberatory critical consciousness, empowerment, and social justice advocacy.

In groups characterized by naïveté, the group focuses only on intrapsychic factors and pays little if any attention to multicultural issues. The social roots of people's behavior and the social justice, human rights implications of such issues are not addressed. In groups characterized by multicultural integration, group leaders help group members understand the importance of the effects of cultural variables on their behavior. The group begins to take on an interpersonal quality. Issues of difference and diversity are beginning to be explored as the group members move from looking only at their own motivations and concerns to becoming concerned with the experiences of other group members. During this phase, group leaders can help members develop an increased capacity to form successful relationships with others.

In the liberatory critical consciousness phase, the group leader helps members understand the social and structural roots of their own personal problems. By so doing, "clients who begin to understand their lives in context in an unjust society have a cognitive and emotional awakening" (Ratts & Santos, 2010, p. 164).

The authors appropriately connect this phase to the important work of Freire (1993) and his exploration of conscientization—the development of an understanding of the roots of one's oppression, which leads to action.

In the following stage, empowerment, the group focuses on helping members move from this consciousness to developing ways of interacting with the oppressive social world. During this phase, explorations of individual pathology largely disappear and are replaced by a discourse of action. The antidote to depression is therefore not psychotherapy or medication but an individual's growing sense of wellness and holiness as they work toward less oppressive interactions with their social worlds.

In the final stage, social justice advocacy, group members plan and conduct social change activities to help change the structural and systemic roots of their oppression. By so doing, they develop a sense of self-efficacy and liberation, while working to make the social environment less oppressive through their collective action.

As mentioned, these are not natural phases that groups pass through but instead are stages that group leaders can consciously lead their group members toward. This demands a shift from intrapsychic views of human behavior to ones that critically assess the social factors that lead to oppression. Such a model encourages facilitating and developing group dynamics that lead toward social change; this model therefore can be an important tool not only for macro level group workers but for all helpers who work with oppressed and marginalized populations. In chapter 13, we explore the importance of group work undertaken from an anti-oppressive perspective. This model is highly congruent with this approach and can be used as a guide to help group workers develop antioppressive practices. Of course, not all social workers or social agencies would view this type of liberational practice as a goal. While this is certainly a valid perspective, we do suggest that attending to this model can help social workers guard against the medicalization of social problems and the increasing tendency to blame individuals for social concerns. Group leaders are in the perfect position, through this type of practice, to challenge what can be a false dichotomy between micro and macro practice (Austin, Coombs, & Barr, 2005).

Yalom's Therapeutic Factors

As we have previously mentioned, not all theories of group processes and dynamics focus on discrete stages. Perhaps the most influential of these approaches is advocated by Yalom, whose therapeutic factors provide us with valuable insights into the dynamics of various treatment groups.

Yalom's (2005) therapeutic factors are very useful ideas for group workers. Yalom's model is perhaps most universally applied to clinical group work yet has important implications for most direct practice groups. In a sense, these therapeutic factors can be used as tools through which to assess the strengths and limitations of a particular group. The worker can use them as a guide for practice by consciously seeking ways of increasing the expression of each therapeutic factor, or as tools for periodic assessment by determining the degree to which each factor is present in the group, and the degree to which each group should be characterized by each factor.

Instillation of hope. Clients often come to treatment feeling hopeless. Social workers often encounter clients at their emotional and physical low points. Groups should help members feel hopeful. Hope and the expectancy of change are powerful therapeutic factors. Hope, in fact, may be an important factor underpinning the placebo effect—when people are positive and believe they can change, they are often on the way to healing and change.

Universality. Universality, or the "all-in-the-same-boat" phenomenon, is important for individuals and for the group as a whole. Universality means helping people feel part of a whole, that their problems are shared by others, and that while they may be different and unique, they are not alone. The feeling of universality helps decrease group members' shame. Too often, group members believe that they are the only ones who have failed in the ways that they have, and their pain and their secrets make them feel isolated. Helping group members share their common problems and concerns not only helps individuals but is an important step in creating group cohesion and goodwill.

Imparting information. At times, helping professionals discount the importance of providing clients with accurate information about their concerns. It is often assumed that for growth or change to occur, deep psychological insights or powerful systems changes need to occur. However, at times, group members' exchange of good information can lead to significant change. One valuable technique that helps clients share information is for the group leader to assign a research project on the problem, and for each member to report back to the group.

Altruism. Being supportive and giving to others are powerful and healing not only for the person receiving help, but for the person giving it. In fact, it may be one of the main reasons why many of us decided to be helping professionals (Dass & Gorman, 1985). People seem to grow and change when they give to others. Group members often report that helping others allows them to heal from their own problems. At the least, those who provide support and encouragement to others will feel more connected to the group, and perhaps less isolated in general.

The corrective recapitulation of the family experience. People bring to the group faulty messages they receive from their families of origin about others and themselves. As such, the group can be a wonderful laboratory in which group members can be encouraged to challenge faulty perceptions. Yalom posits that the group becomes the context through which members can heal the painful experiences they had as members of their families of origin. Group members can learn, for example, that they are worthy of love and caring, and that people will treat them differently from how they were previously treated.

Development of socializing techniques. Not only can people develop new insights about their relationships with people, but they can also practice the behaviors that will help them meet their social aims. Social skills training, role-playing, and encouraging outside practice of social skills can be powerful tools for facilitating the growth of group members.

Imitative behavior. The principle of imitative behavior is based upon social learning theory. In using this principle, group leaders focus on the behavioral principles of behavior shaping and modification. Workers can model desired behaviors and validate the behaviors they observe in group members that are congruent with healthy group dynamics. Behavior shaping not only validates desired behaviors but enables group members to take small steps toward desired behaviors and goals. In working with children in groups, it is important that group workers understand which children are viewed as most powerful or popular by other children, so that they can reinforce desired behaviors and extinguish difficult group behaviors.

Interpersonal learning. Groups are laboratories for interpersonal learning. Group members engage in an ongoing process of relearning their roles, values, and needs in relation to others. Group members have the opportunity to learn new social skills and develop new means of meeting their needs in the context of their relationships with others. As people work toward change, the group becomes a wonderful place where they can experiment with new ways of acting and being. Group member feedback, both formal and informal, becomes valuable information that members can bring with them to real-world situations. To encourage interpersonal learning, group leaders can encourage experimentation and constructive feedback.

Group cohesiveness. Without group cohesion, the group is in trouble. Group cohesion refers to the sense that members are on the same team. In cohesive groups, differences are recognized and reconciled. A cohesive group is almost like a healthy family, in that there is recognition that even when problems exist, members need to be there for one another. Workers can facilitate group cohesion by validating supportive behavior, adopting a warm and empathic tone, positively confronting divisive and harmful behavior, and being clear about the importance of group members supporting each other.

Catharsis. Catharsis, the letting out of intense emotions, can be a powerful experience when it is done in group. It is important that as a group leader you understand your group's dynamics and make certain that the group is ready to respond in a positive manner. When a member presents a great deal of emotion, the group leader is encouraged to model acceptance and unconditional positive regard. The worker focuses on making sure that the group responds without judgment, and without trying to immediately rescue the person from his or her intense emotional expression.

Jacobs's Generic Factors

Jacobs, Masson, and Harvill (2001) provide a less theoretical, more nuts-and-bolts approach to looking at what makes groups work. They note that each of the following factors must be congruent with best practice in group work and the needs of individual groups. To Jacobs et al., the most important factors in the health of a group are the clarity of purpose and the degree to which all other factors are aligned with this purpose.

Clarity of purpose for leader and members. Many authors have argued that establishing and maintaining purpose is one of the most important things a group leader can do. It may seem obvious, yet it is very easy for groups to shift and change over time, without members or leaders being clear about these changes. It is helpful for group leaders to be clear about the purpose of the group, which involves providing members with a sense of the purpose of each activity or section of an individual group session.

Relevance of purpose to members. Of course, the purpose of the group, group sessions, and activities has to correspond to the perceived needs of the group. For this reason, it is often helpful to do periodic assessments of the members' perceptions of whether their needs are being met. Prescreening is also a valuable tool when group leaders are determining if the stated purpose of the group will correspond to the needs and strengths of individual group members.

Size of group. The size of a group is important and depends on the type of group, the group members, and the purpose of the group. Therapy, support, and growth groups should usually be small, in order to support intensive discussion and dialogue. Educational and psychoeducational groups may be larger. Just what are the ideal sizes for some types of groups? While there is no ideal number, there are some guidelines. Therapy and support groups for adults should have between six and ten members, and for children, between four and six. Psychoeducational groups can be a bit larger. Task groups can vary greatly in size, but task groups and committees that work intensively together should not have more than six people. Large task groups can work well if the groups are divided into subgroups or broken into dyads and triads.

Length of each session. Length of group sessions is also an important factor in the success of a group. For instance, a ninety-minute behavioral modification and skills training group with hyperactive grade school boys is bound to fail. This group would likely be far more successful if it were thirty minutes in length. On the other hand, a half-hour therapy group with high-functioning, highly verbal adults is not likely to provide enough time for in-depth discussion. Such a group may be as long as an hour and a half. At times, intensive therapy groups may be as long as several hours, or several hours each day over the course of a week-end. While such long sessions are appealing in that they tend to lead to a high degree of intensity, they should be followed up with more regularly scheduled meetings to ensure that the insights that are made are followed up on in members' day-to-day lives.

Frequency of meetings. How often to hold meetings is also an important decision but one that is often made by default, in that it is assumed that once a week is a good schedule for many types of groups. However, the number of sessions chosen can be a valuable tool in shaping the life of a group. Intensive programs such as inpatient treatment facilities for substance abuse or for persons suffering from acute psychiatric episodes frequently have daily group therapy meetings. The same is true for psychosocial rehabilitation programs, or group homes, which may have very short check-in meetings. Some leaders elect to hold outpatient therapy groups once every other week. However, this can be risky because if a member misses one session, he or she must wait a full month before the next meeting.

Adequacy of setting. When groups are not part of the central functions of a program or agency, group leaders are frequently not given adequate space to run their groups. Groups that are not provided with comfortable and age-appropriate seating and have poor light are not likely to be successful. Group leaders typically forget to assess the impact of the environment on the dynamics of the group, instead focusing on more psychology-related variables. However, if social work has taught us anything, it is that services and lives can be improved with changes to the physical environment.

Time of day. Time is an essential element in social work practice. The time at which a group is held is an important consideration. First and foremost, groups should be held when the targeted client group is available. Poor working adults may not be able to attend a group during nine-to-five hours. On the other hand, many people work evenings and during the night. Group workers who conduct groups in school settings must pay careful attention to the times when their groups are offered, so as to keep disruptions to children's schooling to a minimum. In addition to actual availability, group leaders must take into consideration the varying amounts of energy that people have throughout the day. Both group leaders and group members have times when they function well. While it is rare that group leaders can make the primary scheduling consideration fit with their own energy needs, group leaders must be aware of their natural rhythms. If a group must be scheduled at a time of day when the worker is not typically at his or her best, the worker can make sure to take care of his or her own biopsychosocial needs in order to be as present for the group as possible.

Leader's attitude. Leaders often underestimate the degree to which their own behavior influences the group. This may be due to the frequent use of the term *facilitator*, which does not express the full significance of the group leader to the tone and culture of the group setting. Group members pick up subtle (or not so subtle) clues about the leader's feelings toward groups in general, toward his or her particular group, and toward individual members. This is one of the most important reasons why leaders must learn to be self-reflective.

In general, a group leader should adopt a tone of calm enthusiasm, support, and interest. This does not mean, however, that group leaders should adopt the same emotional stance for all groups. For instance, being overly passive may not be good for some groups, and having too much energy might not work for others.

Closed versus open group. Depending upon the setting and context of the group, groups can be open to new membership or closed after the first session. An example of a group with open membership would be an inpatient psychoeducational group for cardiac patients. In such a group, some patients would only stay for a short period of time, so it would be impossible to have a fixed group for a specified period of time. Closed groups are appropriate when membership will be stable over a given time. Closed groups tend to develop more intimacy than open groups and can more easily move through the developmental phases of group life. A therapy group for incest survivors is one example of a group that should be a closed group.

Voluntary or involuntary membership. Group participants may range from totally voluntary members to those mandated to attend by the legal system. Voluntary members have a different level and type of commitment than do nonvoluntary members. In addition, not all those who are viewed as voluntary members feel their participation is indeed optional. For instance, a husband whose wife tells him he needs to attend a group or she will leave him technically has a choice but may not feel that he does. With such members, it is important to validate their ambivalence so they can come to feel part of the group.

Members' level of commitment. Group commitment can also vary. Group leaders must work to ensure that members are committed to the life of the group. They can do this by helping group members view the group as potentially helpful as quickly as possible. Being hopeful and confident goes a long way toward this aim. Additionally, allowing group members a safe place to share their ambivalence about their commitment is often helpful, provided that the leader is able to keep the conversation moving in a positive direction.

Level of trust among members. Trust exercises are perhaps the most common form of group activity. The ubiquitous nature of these exercises demonstrates the importance of group trust. However, these exercises all too often fail to develop trust. Trust is not something that one can will into being; it must be earned. The leader can work toward developing trust by helping members respond to each other in a helpful, strengths-based, positive manner. As members see that group members and the leader are on their team, they begin to develop a sense of hope and trust in each other.

Members' attitudes toward leaders. There are many reasons why group members may come to feel positively or negatively about a group leader. What is commonly referred to as transference, in which group members respond to the group leader as if he or she is a significant person from their past, is one important influence. Preconceived ideas about the racial or ethnic identity of the group leader, or about his or her gender, may also influence the feelings of group members. Regardless of the reason for these feelings, group leaders must become acutely aware of how their group members feel about them. Group members who are negatively predisposed to the leader or who come to develop negative feelings about the leader over time can be highly disruptive to the group process. On the other hand, a skillful group leader who is able to help group members explore their feelings and behavior and come to an emotional experience of resolve can help members heal many wounds from the past.

Leader's readiness and experience with groups. As with all things in life, there is no substitute for experience in group work. Over time, you will find that your group work skills improve. However, while experience is certainly important, there is no reason why you, as a beginner, cannot run a successful group. All groups have challenging moments, when even the most experienced leader struggles. With patience, calm, centeredness, and the use of good social work skills, leading a group can be a wonderful experience.

Co-leader harmony. Social work interns and beginning social workers often complain about co-leading groups with more senior staff with whom they are not compatible. Co-leadership of groups can be a fantastic way of maximizing the strengths and resources of an agency and can be a powerful tool in training developing practitioners. However, co-leaders should spend considerable time together planning for and ultimately processing their groups. Group leaders must discuss stylistic and ideological issues before a group starts and must continue with such discussion throughout the life of the group. A good general guideline is for group leaders to spend at least fifteen minutes together prior to the start of each group session, and at least the same amount of time afterward. Co-leaders need to develop a good enough working relationship such that they are perceived by group members as being supportive of each other. Co-leaders do not always need to agree, but they must have respect for each other and be clear about the nature of their differences and accept and value each other's skills and abilities.

Working with interpreters. Throughout this book we present ideas and examples of how social workers can use groups with different populations. As we mentioned previously, as a result of globalization, social workers must learn how to work with people who do not have mastery of English. In such situations, social workers must either speak the language of their client or work with interpreters. Unfortunately, too few social workers have the linguistic abilities to work with a variety of different populations. Even those who do speak another language will at some point be called upon to work with those whose language they do not speak. In such situations, social workers work with interpreters. The best interpreters are professionally trained interpreters who understand the dynamic of translation and are skilled in translating for the helping professions. These rare professionals understand the importance of providing literal and contextual translations, checking out interpretations with the worker, and maintaining neutrality. Unfortunately, social workers must often call upon untrained interpreters. Sometimes family members are asked to translate. The use of community and family members presents a number of difficulties. For instance, untrained community members may not wish to translate sensitive things that may reflect poorly on their people. Using family members may lead to the communication of inaccurate information as well and may place family members in difficult situations. In group work, these complex dynamics are intensified. However, the advantage of translation in groups is that other members can verify the accuracy of messages and can provide context on a group level. Research is needed as to the specific strengths, limitations, and dynamics of translation in group work. Group workers working with non-English speakers should advocate for their agencies to seek as many trained interpreters as necessary.

Self-Reflection and Experiential Learning

One of the key principles of this book is that group work must be learned experientially. Through experiential learning, students apply the principles and theories that they learn and integrate them into their behavioral repertoire. In other words, you must learn to make theories of your own. In order to do so, students must develop the ability to be self-reflective about their own use of skills, knowledge, and values and develop the capacity to apply them to various situations. Experiential learning, and self-reflection about this learning, allows students to make knowledge their own. However, self-reflection does not just happen. Students must be taught skills and processes that help them reflect on their reactions to various information and situations. The exercises in this book were designed to do just that.

Self-reflection, particularly about one's own practice skills and behavior, is important for several reasons. First, it is through self-reflection that a practitioner develops the capacity to understand his or her emotional responses to clients, and to the difficult situations that occur when we practice (Furman, Langer, & Anderson, 2006). In other words, our personal "stuff" and emotional baggage invariably affect how we are and how we act. In social work practice, we are the tool of intervention, and we must understand how this tool responds under emotional duress. Second, it is through self-reflection that a practitioner can adopt theory to new and novel practice situations. For example, a group worker who understands how cognitive theory can be used with one group must be able to engage in a critical analysis of that theory in order to apply it to another population.

DeRoos (1990) defines reflection in practice, or reflecting in action, as "the conscious evaluation of action during the course of action" (p. 283). In other words, one needs to pay attention to both one's client and oneself. This is especially challenging when the client is a group, in which social workers must pay attention to the group as a whole (group dynamics) and to individuals (intrapersonal dynamics). Learning to think about one's thinking, feelings, and actions while a group is in session demands that social workers develop several skills. First, as we have said, you must integrate skills into your behavioral repertoire so they become almost second nature. Second, you must develop the capacity to identify your thoughts and feelings. This is not as easy as it sounds, especially in stressful practice situations. Third, you need to learn to be mindful and reflective. This demands a good deal of calm and centeredness. It is one reason that we teach relaxation methods in this book, as they can be of value to clients and for practitioner use.

Chapter 2
Planning for Groups

Before meeting with group members for the first time, social workers should spend considerable time planning for the group. Planning involves defining the purpose, setting, format, content, and composition of the group. Pre-group planning pays off later when group members come together and feel that the group leader has a clear sense of what the group can offer its members and how it will be conducted.

One of the most important aspects for group leaders to plan is the overall group purpose. Often the social worker or the agency he or she works for establishes the purpose of the group and then advertises for potential members to join. The group leader can refine the group purpose once the group begins by involving the group members in exploring their needs and their expectations for the group. Establishing a statement of purpose prior to the first session is a challenging task, as it should encompass the goals of every member but not be so vague or abstract that members do not understand why they are coming together (Northen & Kurland, 2001). The group purpose is guided by the needs of its members.

In designing a group, the social worker should consider the setting and context in which the group will take place. Groups often take place within a broader institution, such as a community agency, a school, or a residential facility. When this is the case, it is important to consider whether the broader organization will support group work as a format for helping clients and whether the purpose of the group is aligned with the mission of the organization. Social workers may need to advocate for the creation of certain types of groups. Logistical planning is necessary to make sure the group will be conducted in an appropriate space and at a convenient time. While this appears to be common sense, finding a location and time that are convenient for potential group members is critical in eliciting their commitment to attend.

The social worker should also think about who will be included in the group and why. To make these decisions, the social worker must carefully consider which potential group members' needs are most likely to fit with the established purpose of the group (Steinberg, 2004). For example, if the group will involve discussion of difficult or sensitive sexual issues, such as victimization, the group may be more successful if it is limited to one gender. If the group will require certain developmental maturities, the group leader may need to designate an age requirement for inclusion; dividing up youths by school level (elementary, middle, and high school) often results in more cohesive groups.

Another consideration in planning for groups is the ideal group size. This may depend, in part, on the type of group one is running. Psychoeducational groups, where members are learning information in a classroom-like environment, may include more group members than therapeutic groups, which require more time to process each member's emotions and thoughts. In making these decisions, the leader should strive for a balance—the group should be small enough to give everyone time to participate actively, but large enough to benefit from multiple perspectives. Smaller groups are likely to have fewer communication difficulties and are less complex, but larger groups allow for a multitude of problem-solving ideas (Zastrow, 2005). Groups can be either open, in which new people can continuously join the group as they like, or closed, in which new members can no longer join once a certain number of people have joined or after the first couple of sessions. The leader should think through how these designations could affect the functioning of the group and should make decisions based on what will best meet the needs of the group members and the organization.

The group leader can also plan for the group by thinking through the structure of the group (Steinberg, 2004). The structure includes what will be done in the group, by whom, and when. Will group sessions involve activities, exercises, use of media, role-playing, or demonstrations of skills? Will the group begin and end in any certain way? For example, groups may begin with a check-in, during which each group member is given time to share briefly how he or she is doing or bring up topics he or she would like to discuss. It is also important to consider and be prepared to explain specific theories that will guide the group process. For example, if the group leader practices from a behavioral perspective, he or she should describe this theory to the group and explain how this influences the type of active practice that will be done in the group. When group leaders have thought through these questions about group structure and design, it is easier for potential group members to decide whether the content fits their expectations and needs. Some group leaders, however, may also choose to adjust the group structure once it begins and incorporate feedback from group members.

The ultimate goal in preparing for a group is to develop a forum that will be comfortable and will help meet the needs of potential group members around a particular issue. Leaders should anticipate group members' capacities for communication and sharing when developing a group (Steinberg, 2004). For most groups, it takes some time for members to become comfortable with one another, and the group leader should spend some time identifying ways to increase comfort and overcome challenges to communication. For example, group leaders may pay particular attention to arranging the room in a way that allows for interaction among all members and may plan icebreaker exercises to encourage communication among members.

Exercises

Assessing Sponsorship and Potential Membership

Objective

To learn to evaluate agency sponsorship as it affects group membership

Writing and Reflection

Assessing agency sponsorship for groups and potential membership of groups are related issues. Think of the social service agency that you know best. If you have yet to work in a social service agency, you may use your school of social work for this exercise.

1. What are the unmet needs of this agency's clients?

   _____

2. What type of group might help meet these needs?

   _____

3. Describe the fit between the mission of the agency and the type of group you are thinking of creating.

   _____

4. What resources do you need to start the group?

   _____

5. Who can help you secure the needed resources?

   _____

6. Who might be resistant to starting this group? Why might he or she be resistant?

   _____

7. How can you help this person become invested in the group?

   _____

8. Describe the clients who may be potential members of this group.

   _____

9. What would be a good way of describing your group to clients so that they will be interested in attending?

   _____

Practice in Planning

Objectives

- To develop your ability to plan various types of groups
- To develop your ability to work collaboratively in the planning process

In-Class Exercise

To practice the planning process, you will be developing groups that would have been helpful after the tragedy of September 11, 2001. You will work in teams of four to design groups to work with the following client populations.

- Muslim or Middle Eastern students on your campus
- Schoolchildren whose parents died in the tragedy
- Witnesses to the tragedy who now suffer from anxiety and stress
- Social work professionals wanting to discuss what can be done about the tragedy

You will want to decide upon a structure for the group as a whole, as well as a detailed outline of the first session. In constructing the format, take into account all the issues you have learned about planning groups. You will obviously have to account for group size, length of sessions, number of sessions, type of group, and format, as well as many other factors.

1. Important issues to consider

_____

2. Overall structure of group

_____

3. First session plan

_____

4. Final session plan

_____

Group Planning Checklist

1. What is the purpose of the group?
2. Group composition
    - Sometimes selection criteria are a luxury.
    - Do you have a good mix of personalities (e.g., not all shy people or all loud people)?
    - Have you, if possible, assessed the appropriateness of each individual for the type of group you are conducting?

3. What is your target group size? (Groups should be large enough to yield a variety of opinions, yet small enough to foster a sense of belonging where everyone has a chance to participate.)

   ■ For preadolescents, three to four participants is workable.

   ■ For adolescents, groups should consist of six to ten members.

   ■ For adults, groups should have seven to ten members.

   ■ Have you anticipated nonattendance and dropouts?

4. Will there be one leader or co-leaders?

   The use of co-leaders brings the benefit of coverage of the group in case one leader is unavailable. Also, one leader can scan the group (see p. 52 for a discussion of scanning) for nonverbal communication while the other leader is focusing on the conversation. They can also play "good cop/bad cop" by having one leader confront unhealthy behaviors and the other leader provide supportive help enabling participants to work through that confrontation. The benefit of single leadership is that it is more cost effective and less confusing to members, who may grapple with the question of who is in charge.

5. What will be the duration of the group meetings?

   ■ For adults, one-and-a-half to two hours is ideal.

   ■ For children and adolescents, a shorter length is appropriate due to shorter attention spans.

6. What will be the frequency of the meetings?

   In an institutional setting, daily meetings are often possible and desirable. If members are drawn from the community, weekly or monthly meetings are most realistic.

7. Where will the group meet?

   The meeting place should be quiet, private, comfortable (right temperature, nice chairs), and large enough to accommodate a circle of chairs.

8. When will the group meet?

   There is never a time that accommodates everyone's needs and wants. Therefore, the leader should decide on a time that appears to work for the majority of the members. However, in deciding when to meet, leaders should take into consideration family and work responsibilities. Sometimes it is appropriate to hold one group during work hours and another during evening hours.

9. How many times will the group meet?

   This number is tied to purpose. Some groups, like skills and informational groups, meet only once or twice, and others, like support and treatment groups are unlimited in duration. Most groups, however, should be time limited (such as three, six, or ten meetings). This helps members and the leader or co-leaders plan their time, prepare for termination, and not drag on without a purpose.

10. Will the group be open or closed?

    The group leader can make this decision or allow the group members to make the decision at the first or second group meeting. Advantages of open groups are that new members bring fresh perspectives and they benefit from the experience of the members who have been participating longer. Advantages of closed groups are that they build trust and cohesion more quickly and are able to achieve a greater level of intensity because of it.

11. Is the group for voluntary or involuntary clients, or both?

    Involuntary members may be forced by court order to attend group meetings but cannot be made to interact in meaningful and productive ways. Leaders of groups with all involuntary members must work diligently to confront resistant and manipulative behaviors. The leaders of mixed groups should work to ensure that involuntary clients do not spoil the group experience for those who choose to attend.

12. What will the group rules be?

    In addition to group norms that form as the group gets underway, the leader should set at least a few group rules in order to protect the healthy functioning of the group. Examples of possible group rules are:

    - Members are expected to attend all meetings.
    - Members are expected to maintain confidentiality. "What is said in the group stays in the group."
    - Members cannot smoke or drink alcohol during the group.
    - Members cannot stay and participate in a group when they arrive under the influence of drugs or alcohol.
    - Members who are minors must have parents' written consent to participate.
    - Members are to avoid dating or having sexual relationships with fellow group members.
    - Members who make threats or engage in sexual harassment will be excluded (Sheafor, Horejsi, & Horejsi, 1994).

13. What activities will happen with regularity at meetings?

    Icebreakers, refreshments, introductions, round-robins, open discussion, structured discussion, guest speaker, role-playing, reminder of next meeting, homework assignments

14. How will you handle practical problems?

   ■ What happens if members arrive late, too many people arrive and there is not enough space, the leader must miss a meeting, there is very bad weather, members bring uninvited friends, conflicts arise between members outside group?

   ■ Who pays for refreshments?

Chapter 3
Beginning

The primary purpose of the beginning stage of groups is group formation. This phase can be stress provoking for group leaders and group members alike. Group members are deciding how committed they will be to participating, and how much they trust the leader and other group members. Understandably, group members are often guarded at the beginning of group, often feeling self-conscious and uncertain as they cautiously engage. This beginning phase can also create anxiety for leaders, who want group members to value the group and actively participate. Group leaders should expect some discomfort but confidently rely on the preparation they have done before group to guide them. Leaders should also be aware of their own reactions to the group and its members and identify ways to connect with each member. It is especially important for the group leader to take an active and directive role during the beginning phase of group (Northen & Kurland, 2001). Group leaders need to facilitate introductions, establish the purpose of the group, help the group set rules and norms, and begin to establish rapport with members.

As in any new beginning, groups should begin with introductions. The leader will often begin introductions by sharing his or her credentials, experience as a group leader, and hopes for the group. In doing so, the leader should establish his or her competence as a group leader while also being transparent about his or her own expectations. This is the time when the group leader orients the members to the group, clearly stating the purpose of the group. While leaders are often apprehensive about being too assertive with their own ideas for the group, it is important that he or she explicitly state the purpose of the group by sharing the overall goal of group participation. This will give the group a focus and get members on the same page, while leaving room for group members to ask questions and make suggestions.

Components of this orientation include the establishment of rules, norms, and roles. The setting of ground rules, such as maintaining confidentiality and having respectful interactions, offers group members a sense of safety and security and ultimately results in a more cohesive and productive group. Members can take ownership of the group by participating in developing the group rules and norms. Group norms, including starting the group on time, bringing refreshments, and sharing time among group members, can be openly discussed by the group. Seeking agreement on these norms means that group members can hold each other accountable for upholding the norms of the group.

The leader should clearly state his or her perceived role in the group. As discussed later in this book, different types of groups may require leaders to play different roles. The group leader may thus see himself or herself as a teacher, a facilitator, or a listener, or in a host of other roles. The leader may also see his or her primary responsibilities as sharing information or expertise with the group, making connections between group members, reflecting overall themes discussed in group, or attempting to develop insight into group members' behaviors. The leader should be open to explaining this role and the types of topics and exercises he or she plans to use to fulfill that role. Group members' roles in group will be affected by the purpose of the group, the role of the leader, and individual members' comfort levels. Ideally, the group members will both seek help from the group and offer help to others.

Group members should be given time to introduce themselves and begin to build rapport. Often adding structure to this introductory phase makes group members feel more comfortable and elicits more active participation. For example, leaders can establish a round-robin format, in which group members go around the circle, taking turns introducing themselves and sharing where they are from, why they are joining the group, what they hope to get out of the group, and something enjoyable they did the previous weekend. This type of structure allows the leader and other members to get a sense of the group's needs as well as get to know each other on a personal level in a nonthreatening way. Round-robin formats can be adapted for each session to encourage group members to begin discussing particular topics pertinent to the purpose of each group session.

With time, group members should become more comfortable with one another and require fewer imposed structures to share their thoughts and feelings. During the beginning phase, however, the group leader should develop a number of different icebreakers to help the group members get to know one another. Games can be used to introduce the group members and identify common feelings and experiences. These activities can provide a format for group members to let their guards down (Zastrow, 2005). During rapport building, the leader strives to strike a balance between conveying a sense of empathy, caring, and neutrality and being assertive and sharing his or her valuable knowledge. Modeling these qualities will help members develop a sense of trust in the group (Northen & Kurland, 2001).

The beginning stage of group is used to establish comfort among members while giving members a clear sense of what the group will involve. How a leader conducts himself or herself in the first few group sessions will set a tone for the group, including how serious and formal or structured or flexible the group will be. The primary goals of this beginning stage should be to orient and connect group members. Rather than expecting members to share deep emotions, the leader should focus on identifying mutual experiences among members (Glassman & Kates, 1990). Group leaders should thus seek to create an atmosphere of support and comfort appropriate for exploring the needs of the group.

Exercises

Opening a Group

Objective

To develop your ability to open groups, using a variety of skills

In-Class Exercise

In a group of six to eight students, take turns opening a group. You may role-play a treatment group for men who have been convicted of spousal abuse or develop your own group. The main purpose of the suggested group is to help the men learn to control their behavior.

The purpose of this exercise is to practice different ways of opening groups and then assess what worked and what did not. Remember, group leaders must give clear directions for what they want group members to do and discuss. Use the following formats for opening the group.

1. *Dyads.* Members break into pairs for introduction to explore their expectations. Dyads are useful ways of encouraging all members of a group to communicate and work. Since dyads consist of two people, they replicate comfortable and familiar communication patterns.

2. *Round-robins.* Members of the group take turns responding to requests for information. The leader can ask members to provide a word that describes how they feel about participating in a group, a 1–10 rating of how comfortable they are, or any other pertinent information. Round-robins are a quick and useful way of obtaining valuable information.

3. *An exercise.* Exercises can set the tone of action and participation in a group.

4. *Statement of purpose and goals.* The leader opens the group by discussing the expectations, procedure, and norms of the group.

Writing and Reflection

1. Which of these openings seemed to work the best for you? Why?

_____

2. Describe something that one of your fellow students did that you would like to incorporate into your style.

_____

Establishing Group Purpose

Objective

To learn to establish clarity about the purpose of a group

Written Exercise

Describe three ways you would establish purpose in each of the following situations.

1. A school-based psychoeducational group for parents with elementary school children diagnosed with ADHD

_____

2. A community-based task group with various constituencies gathering to discuss community opinions and concerns about a proposed chemical plant in the neighborhood

_____

3. An inpatient therapy group for battered women

_____

In-Class Exercise

With a partner, practice the statements that you developed. Give each other feedback about your statements of purpose.

Writing and Reflection

1. What did you like about your partner's statements of purpose? What would you change about your partner's statements of purpose?

_____

2. What were the strengths of how your partner delivered his or her statements of purpose?

_____

3. What would you like to incorporate into your own practice about the way your partner delivered his or her statements of purpose? What would you change about your delivery?

_____

4. Based upon the feedback you received from your partner, what would you change about your statements of purpose?

_____

5. Based upon this feedback, what would you change about your delivery?

_____

Cohesion

Objective

To develop an understanding of the factors that lead to group cohesion

Writing and Reflection

Group cohesion is essential for optimal group functioning. People often affiliate with groups to meet social needs that are not being met in other areas of their lives. Proper group cohesion can lead to better outcomes, as people become more invested in the group experience. Group leaders must constantly work toward building cohesion, often called the "all-in-the-same-boat" phenomenon. Spend some time addressing the following reflection questions related to group cohesion.

1. Think about group experiences you have had where the group members exhibited a high degree of cohesion. What was the group like? What were the behaviors of the group leader that helped you feel close to and part of the group? What were the behaviors of your fellow group members that contributed to this feeling?

2. Think about group experiences you have had where group members exhibited a low degree of cohesion. What was the group like? What were the behaviors of the group leader that led to poor cohesion? What were the behaviors of your fellow group members that contributed to this feeling?

Tuning in to Nonverbal Communication

Objective

To develop an understanding of nonverbal communication

Communication experts assert that 90 percent of all face-to-face communication is nonverbal, and that up to 50 percent of that nonverbal communication is conveyed by facial expressions, and 30 percent by voice inflection and tone (Sheafor et al., 1994). By paying very close attention to group members' nonverbal communication, the group leader can monitor how clients appear to be feeling and determine if their nonverbal communication matches what they are saying.

In-Class Exercise

In small groups, conduct a short group session about a topic of mutual interest, such as how to reduce stress and burnout in college. Each group member should monitor the nonverbal communication of the other group members around the following parameters.

1. *Eye contact.* Lack of eye contact can indicate a lack of interest. Glaring or staring can signify rudeness or anger. Remember, various cultures have different norms concerning eye contact.

2. *Tone of voice.* Tone of voice reveals feelings. Loud or forceful tone reveals aggressiveness, control, or strength; meek or quiet voice tone can mean fear or withdrawal. A monotone voice usually indicates a lack of interest or depressed mood.

3. *Facial expressions.* Expressions such as frowning, smiling, scowling, a quivering lip, and blushing all indicate how the client is feeling.

4. *Body language.* Crossed legs and folded arms or hands usually indicate defensiveness. Clenched fists indicate anger, and fidgeting, leg bouncing, and hand tapping can mean impatience or nervousness.

5. *Dress and overall appearance.* Notice each group member's appearance at each meeting to see if you notice differences. Typically, people who are feeling better about themselves and their life situations tend to their appearance and dress more, but there are exceptions to this pattern.

Group leaders need to pay close attention to their own dress and appearance because these elements communicate to clients who you are and how you feel. Make sure your dress is not offensive to group members. For example, a group of adolescents at a youth center may not object to you wearing blue jeans, but a group of older adults in a church-based setting might (Sheafor et al., 1994).

After meeting as a group for at least ten minutes, end your group process and come together as classroom colleagues to discuss the nonverbal communication you observed. See what nonverbal communication most members noticed. See what was noticed by only a few. What nonverbal communication did group members receive from you? Do you agree that you were sending these nonverbal messages?

Chapter 4
Working: Dynamics and Leadership

In the middle phase of group, members have developed rapport, feel more comfortable with one another, and are able to do more work. Whether the goal of the group is to learn new information, develop new skills, support one another, or change feelings or behaviors, the middle stage is focused on goal achievement. In this phase, certain components of groups, such as group dynamics and leadership techniques, become especially important. The group's hard work is often accompanied by certain challenges and conflicts that should be addressed in this phase of the group process.

Every social work group leader must develop his or her own leadership style. As leaders gain experience and recognize their own strengths and weaknesses, they become more aware of the style that fits best for them. Leadership in groups often involves striking a balance between being too directive and not directive enough. Without leadership, the group is likely to be unproductive at best and, at worst, the most outspoken group members are likely run the group by default (Doel, 2006). On the other hand, group leaders must make sure they do not completely take over the group but instead empower group members and leave room for the group to form its identity and take charge of the change process. Doel suggests leading on behalf of the group; by this he means that leaders can take charge and lead the group until the members are ready to take a more active leadership role. The middle/working phase of the group is often a good time for the leader to begin relinquishing some control or authority and handing it over to group members who are now ready to do the work.

In leading groups, the social worker must decide when to join with the group, participating as a member versus directing the group. The social worker, by virtue of being present in the group at every session, is a part of the group, but participation in activities or sharing should be carefully thought through and may seem more appropriate at certain times than others. For example, if each member sitting in the circle is sharing about his or her hopes for the group, then it may be appropriate and even necessary for the group leader to also share his or her expectations and hopes. Conversely, if all group members are sharing about their challenges with self-doubt, the group leader would probably choose not to join in. While the leader may have feelings about the topic being discussed, or even personal experience, sharing in group should only be done when the leader truly feels that sharing will benefit the group and its members. In situations where it is not appropriate for the group leader to share personal information, he or she can still act as a support and offer knowledge and skills to the group.

Social work group leaders often find it difficult to remove their own emotions from the group when sensitive or personal topics are discussed. However, group leaders are challenged to recognize these emotions and set them aside and focus on the needs of the group. As in other stages of group, the leader continues to reflect on his or her role in the group process. By understanding how his or her own beliefs and emotions can help or interfere with the group, the group leader is more purposeful in interactions during the group process (Northen & Kurland, 2001).

Group cohesion is an important aspect of group dynamics during this working phase. Having used the beginning stages of group to test their ability to trust and confide in the group, members are likely to start feeling they are a part of a cohesive unit. Groups feel especially cohesive when individual members see similarities with one another and when they associate membership in the group with security, resources, and positive outcomes (Toseland, Jones, & Gellis, 2004). As the group becomes more cohesive, it takes on an identity of its own, and this cohesion can lead to more honest and productive communication.

Conflict may arise between group members as they let down their guard and start to deal with difficult issues. Now that group members are less concerned with whether others in the group will like or accept them, they are not afraid to express their differences and talk about serious issues. Group members may disagree with each other's perspectives on problems or might object to others' approaches to problems. The group leader should try to use this conflict as a natural and productive component of group work. Conflict offers an opportunity for the group to problem solve in order to reach resolution, utilizing skills emphasized in group work (Northen & Kurland, 2001). Certain skills are especially necessary for the group leader, including paraphrasing and clarifying members' statements to increase clear communication and mediate disagreements between members (Brandler & Roman, 1999).

In the working phase of group, leaders may confront group members more often than in previous phases of group. Leaders may use confrontation when members are denying their problems, are stuck and not making progress toward their goals, or are providing advice to others but not applying it to themselves, or when they say something offensive or hurtful to another member. Regardless of the reason for confrontation, it is often uncomfortable for social work group leaders. Leaders might feel mean or worry that the group might not like them or trust them after they use confrontation. However, being confronted on an important issue can be a real catalyst for change, and without confrontation, some members may not make progress. Confrontation between group members can be powerful and should be encouraged; however, the leader may be responsible for taking the risk of challenging group members.

The working phase of group can be a very exciting time in the group process. Up to this point, much has been done to build the group's comfort level and set the stage for goal achievement. Now a more cohesive group can challenge its members to make individual and collective progress. This phase of group can be spread out across numerous sessions and may continue until group members complete their goals or until, due to a predetermined group length, the termination process begins.

Exercises

The Purpose of Communication

Objective

To develop your awareness of the motivation for people's verbal and nonverbal communication

Writing and Reflection

Understanding communication is essential for beginning a group. People in groups communicate to address important interpersonal concerns. In this sense, most communication can be understood as designed to meet some psychosocial need. In this exercise, you will explore examples of how people communicate to meet these needs. Please provide examples from your own practice or personal experience, times when you have exhibited or witnessed examples of the types of communication listed below. Provide examples of both verbal and nonverbal communication that are indicative of attempts to meet each communication need.

1. Attempts to demonstrate understanding

   a. Verbal

   _____

   b. Nonverbal

   _____

2. Attempts to understand another's feelings toward you, or how he or she perceives you

   a. Verbal

   _____

   b. Nonverbal

   _____

3. Attempts to persuade someone to meet one's needs

   a. Verbal

   _____

   b. Nonverbal

   _____

4. Attempts to gain or maintain power in communication
   a. Verbal

   _____

   b. Nonverbal

   _____

5. Attempts to defend oneself from others
   a. Verbal

   _____

   b. Nonverbal

   _____

6. Attempts to provide feedback to others
   a. Verbal

   _____

   b. Nonverbal

   _____

7. Attempts to make an impression on others
   a. Verbal

   _____

   b. Nonverbal

   _____

8. Attempts to develop or maintain relationships
   a. Verbal

   _____

   b. Nonverbal

   _____

9. Group members' attempts to express cohesion and unity
   a. Verbal

   _____

   b. Nonverbal

   _____

Co-leadership

Objective

To develop a personal understanding of the benefits and potential pitfalls of co-leadership

In-Class Exercise

Leading a group with another social worker or helping professional can be both helpful and difficult. This exercise is designed to help you understand some of the advantages and difficulties of co-leadership. Form groups of five to eight students. Pairs of students will co-lead the groups for ten minutes. The other group members will play the roles of members of an inpatient drug and alcohol treatment group. The group members will be asked to discuss issues related to their most recent relapses. The group leaders' job is to facilitate discussion. Normally, co-leaders should do considerable planning and discuss potential issues before they lead a group. For the purpose of this assignment, however, the leaders will go into the group cold. The co-leaders should try to support their co-leaders and help facilitate the discussion.

Class Discussion

1. What were the difficulties of co-leading the group?

   _____

2. What were the advantages of co-leading the group?

   _____

3. Based upon this experience, what issues would you have liked to discuss with your co-leader prior to leading this group?

   _____

Writing and Reflection

1. What was it like for you when your co-leader did something you disagreed with? Were you able to accept and support him or her? Did your verbal or nonverbal behavior suggest disagreement? If so, how?

   _____

2. Did you feel supported by your co-leader? Did he or she do anything that made you feel unsupported? If so, what?

   _____

3. How may your own personal issues related to power and control affect your ability to co-lead a group?

_____

4. What do you feel are your strengths related to co-leading groups?

_____

5. What skills do you feel you need to continue to develop in order to be an effective co-leader?

_____

6. List and discuss several steps you will take to improve your co-leadership skills.

_____

Communication and Interactional Patterns: Sending and Receiving Messages

Objective

To develop an understanding of how messages can become distorted in the transmission between sender and receiver

In-Class Exercise

One of the most important ways group leaders facilitate the creation of positive group dynamics is by facilitating healthy patterns of communication. Distortions in communication between the sender and the receiver of the message are common. In this exercise, you will work together in triads, taking turns playing the role of the client, the group worker, and an observer. The client and the worker are to have a dialogue that could occur in a group. The goal is for the student who is role-playing the worker to reflect back to the client, as best he or she can, the meaning of what the client has said. You may use the three scenarios listed below or invent your own.

1. A treatment group for Latino men in an outpatient substance abuse program. Jose just learned that he lost his job and has been feeling like drinking.

_____

2. A psychoeducational group for new mothers. Linda, a nineteen-year-old single mother, is discussing her fears of losing the best years of her life to a new baby and the shame of having these feelings.

_____

3. A community group for neighbors to discuss their feelings about a new group home for homeless mentally ill men that is being planned for the community. Mac is a fifty-year-old man who has lived on the block his whole life.

He is angry that the home is being built on his street but has some empathy for the men.

Writing and Reflection

1. In the role of the worker, what was it like for you when you were not able to fully understand your client?

---

2. In the role of the client, what was it like for you when you were not fully understood by the worker?

---

3. In the role of the observer, what behaviors did you witness that facilitated clear communication?

---

4. In the role of the observer, what behaviors did you witness that seemed to lead to communication problems?

---

5. Reflecting upon this experience, what behaviors or skills would you like to develop?

---

6. List a few action steps that you will use to develop these new behaviors.

Group Dynamics Case Example

Objective

To develop an understanding of group dynamics

Case Example

Jim is a social worker at a community mental health program in a large city. He provides individual and group therapy in an outpatient forensic program. Most of Jim's clients have significant histories of committing violent crimes. The majority of them have spent time in prison. The purpose of the program is to help clients cope with their mental health and substance abuse issues, which are factors that have played significant roles in their violent criminal behaviors.

One of the groups that Jim leads is for female offenders with histories of violent behavior. The group consists of ten members, although Jim prefers his groups to have eight members. Even though these clients are mandated by the legal system to comply with all treatment requirements, including attending group, rarely do all members show up. The group started five sessions ago and is open ended, although actual turnover in the group is anticipated to be relatively low. On most days, between five and seven women show up to the group. A core group of four have attended each of the first sessions.

Jim starts each week by asking the women how they are doing, and if anyone would like to share what happened during the week. He believes that this helps the members of his group take ownership of their own treatment. For the past two weeks, members have not spoken in response to his invitation. He got the sense that Carol wanted to share, but that something stopped her. He remembers a few weeks prior, when Carol was sharing about her incest, she suddenly stopped sharing in the middle of her story. When she stopped, she averted her eyes from one side of the group. One of the members of the group appeared to be staring at her very intently, with a smile on her face that Jim perceived as odd.

Jim decided to conduct a check-in round to see how the members were doing, to get them to share at least some information, and to break what he perceived to be tension in the room. Jim decided to start his round so that it ended on Jill, the woman who was staring so intently at Carol while she spoke of her incest. Jim asked the members to rate how they were feeling and doing this past week on a scale from 1 to 10, 10 being fantastic, 1 being terrible. The majority of the women in the group reported numbers between 3 and 6. Tomika, an African American woman who has a diagnosis of bipolar disorder, reported a 2. Jill reported a 9. When the round ended, Jim asked Tomika if she would like to share about why she scored her week so low. Scanning the group to gauge the responses of the members, Jim noticed that several members were looking at Jill, and that they were shifting uncomfortably in their chairs. Tomika seemed to look at Jill before deciding if she wanted to share or not. Jill immediately said, "Well, I don't think we should talk about people who had bad weeks. I mean, I had a great week, and I think I want to talk about it. Why do we always have to focus on the garbage? I mean, I had a messed up week in some ways, but that's life, why should we talk about it, you know?" Jim thanked Jill for speaking up and told her while he understood her feelings about discussing negative events, and that it was sometimes very painful, he believed that sometimes people need to get things off their chests or get feedback about things so they can change them. Betsy, a young African American woman with a history of sexual abuse, started to laugh uncontrollably. She said that she had the funniest thing happen to her during the week, and something Jill said had reminded her of this. She got up from her chair and quickly started to do an impression of a friend. As Carol began to cry, Jill started to get up and leave the group. Jim asked for everyone to sit down and relax for a few minutes. He said that he felt that the group was going through a hard period, and that it was important to figure out what was going on. He first asked the group if they would take a few minutes to sit in silence and try to "get ourselves together." Jill and Betsy sat down and the group slipped into momentary silence.

Writing and Reflection

Describe your sense of the group dynamics of the preceding case example. The following questions are designed to guide you in your assessment.

1. What can you tell about the nature of the communication and interaction patterns in the group?

   _____

2. Describe your sense of the group's cohesion.

   _____

3. Describe the norms of the group.

   _____

4. Describe the rules of the group.

   _____

5. Discuss various roles different group members play.

   _____

6. How would you describe the culture of the group?

   _____

7. What would it be like to lead such a group?

   _____

8. How might the group leader intervene in order to alter some of the dynamics of this group?

   _____

9. How might the gender of the group leader affect group dynamics, processes, and culture?

   _____

10. Based on this assessment of gender, how should the group leader's behavior differ from that displayed when leading a mixed-gender group or a group of all men?

    _____

Role Reversal Exercise

Objective

To develop creative skills in group work

In-Class Exercise

This activity can be used in treatment, psychoeducational, and other types of groups when it appears that any group members have blind spots affecting the way they interact interpersonally. This technique is helpful when a group member seems to have little awareness of how someone else feels or how he or she comes across to others. Try this activity in small groups in your class.

The group leader initiates the role reversal between two group members by saying something like, "Barbara and Janie, would you be willing to try something different for a few moments? I would like for you two to switch chairs and for a few minutes reverse roles to see how it feels to be the other person." It is important for the group members to switch chairs, or they will get confused as to who they are (Sheafor et al., 1994). Once they are in the role of the other person, the leader can steer the topic to an area where one or the other exhibits a self-defeating behavior, such as repeatedly saying, "Yes, but . . ." to good options offered by the group members. Other self-defeating behaviors that can be acted out are defensiveness, difficulty making decisions, unrealistic mistrust, and feelings of inferiority. Sometimes clients with these self-defeating behaviors greatly benefit from seeing how they interact and react demonstrated for them by a fellow group member. This activity is only effective if the leader keeps the atmosphere lighthearted and no one takes the task too seriously. This helps prevent group members from feeling made fun of. The two people who changed roles should switch back to their original chairs and process what they have seen and learned about themselves by seeing their behaviors and typical verbalizations played out before them.

Writing and Reflection

1. How did you feel about taking on the role of one of your classroom peers? How did you act during the role reversal?

2. How did your peer react to your portrayal of him or her?

3. How were you portrayed by your peer?

4. Did the role reversal give you any insight into how you present yourself?

5. Were you and your classroom peers able to keep the atmosphere lighthearted? If so, how?

Chapter 5
Evaluation

With the growing emphasis placed on empirically based practice in social work, evaluating group work for its effectiveness is essential. Both the group process (what happens during group) and its outcomes (the effects of group participation on members' well-being) should be evaluated to give the group leader, the agency, and the group members a clear understanding of how the group is progressing.

A primary aspect of group evaluation involves asking group members directly about the effects of the group. When conducting an evaluation with group members, the leader should ask broad questions about the strengths of the group, the weaknesses of the group, and ideas for improving the group (Zastrow, 2005) as well as seek feedback about any particular activities or techniques used. This form of evaluation can be done verbally during check-in rounds throughout the course of the group process. Group members, however, may feel pressure to please the group leader by giving desirable answers (Rubin & Babbie, 2008), especially at the beginning of the group process, when the group is still forming and members may be more guarded and less comfortable giving honest feedback. Such check-ins are more likely to elicit useful information midway through the group and in environments where open and genuine dialogue has been established between members and the group leader.

Group leaders may consider seeking feedback about group members' perceptions of the group through anonymous questionnaires to reduce the bias associated with assessment in front of the rest of the group. These types of written evaluations are commonly used in agencies at the conclusion of services. While they provide some indication of group members' level of satisfaction with the group, they do not measure its effectiveness.

To best evaluate the group's effectiveness, group leaders should utilize pre-group and post-group assessments that target the specific thoughts, feelings, and behaviors the group aims to change. To ask such targeted questions, the leader and the group members must have a clear understanding of the purpose of the group and the outcomes desired. A clear purpose directly informs the questions the leader asks at the beginning and end of the group to measure change. For example, a treatment group oriented toward alleviating postpartum depression might use a standardized measure of depressive symptoms at the start of the group to assess members' functioning prior to treatment and then repeat the same measure at the end of the group to see if individuals, and the group as a whole, improved over the course of the group. Depending on the length of the measure and the time it takes to administer it, leaders might also decide to conduct evaluations midway through the group to get a sense of group members' progress and identify ways to improve the second half of the group.

If leaders are designing their own assessment measures instead of using standardized assessment tools, having a clear idea of the purpose and goals of the group is especially important. For example, the leader of a postpartum depression group might want to design questions asking how many days in a given week a group member feels sad, hopeless, or fatigued. The leader might want to inquire about members' feelings toward their children and their perceptions of their ability to parent. Group leaders should carefully construct the questions they ask to avoid confusing or leading questions (Rubin & Babbie, 2008). Asking questions before and after group treatment will give the leader and group members a sense of the progress made toward their goals and help identify issues that still need to be addressed.

Group leaders may also choose to evaluate the group through observation. Group leaders often write progress notes after each group session that document the goal or topic of the individual session, the activities or interventions used, group members' reactions and discussions, and a brief analysis of the session. The leader might make note of techniques that appeared to work well in the group, as well as techniques or activities that fell flat. Observing, writing, and reading progress notes provides the group leader with valuable information and allows him or her to reflect on the progress of the group. The group leader can observe whether the group members seem to be progressing through stages, becoming more comfortable with one another, and making progress toward their common goal. Observations and notes about the process of the group can also help identify particular group members in need of more attention, such as those who are struggling or are especially quiet during group. Understanding these dynamics is difficult while one is conducting the group; thus putting them in writing and reflecting on them between sessions is an important form of evaluation (Northen & Kurland, 2001).

Group leaders should also evaluate themselves over the course of the group. They may ask themselves questions related to different stages of the group process, including how well they met group members' needs during the initial stages of group and their effective use of relationship (ability to provide support to members), choice of interventions (use of skills and different approaches), structure of the group (empowerment of members, establishing norms), and ability to create productive and respectful interactions among group members (Northen & Kurland, 2001). Other forms of evaluation include asking colleagues to observe a group session or videotaping a session that can then be reviewed by a colleague or supervisor, who can provide feedback (Zastrow, 2005).

Evaluating the group process, whether through verbal check-ins, satisfaction surveys, pre-group/post-group assessments, or self-reflection, can create anxiety for group leaders. Group leaders may fear negative feedback or assessments that indicate the group intervention is not working. These are valid and common fears. Yet group leaders must work past these anxieties, because identifying interventions that are not effective and working to improve these interventions is the ethical responsibility of all service providers. Providing services based on the hope or a hunch that they are working is not best serving group members' needs. To improve one's practice and service to others, social workers must seek evaluation of their group work and use that evaluation to actively improve their work. Negative feedback or assessment results, however, should not be taken personally or as indications of failure or incompetence. While the leader should take responsibility for addressing poor evaluations, this could take many different forms, including changing the format of the group, reassessing who is included in the group, or changing the length of the group, the approach, or interactions among members.

Group leaders, especially new leaders, may be surprised at the positive feedback they receive from group members during evaluation. Group leaders should be aware of what they are doing well and should continue to do, in addition to identifying areas for improvement. Furthermore, conducting evaluations during group may be helpful in drawing the group's attention back to the overall purpose and helping individual members reflect on their level of motivation, progress, and efforts toward change.

Exercises
Observing Accurately

Objective

To practice observation

In-Class Exercise

While being able to accurately observe is an important skill in all group work practice, it is essential to the evaluation process. In groups of five or six students, a leader will practice observing certain behaviors. Group members are to simulate a treatment group for persons suffering from low self-esteem. The worker should make note of the number of times group members engage in the following behaviors: sighing, interrupting, exhibiting signs of discomfort, and exhibiting disinterest. Group members should also keep track of how many times they exhibit each behavior, for the sake of comparison. After five minutes, the leader and group members should compare tallies. Each person in the group should take a turn in the role of the leader so that everyone can practice their observation skills.

Writing and Reflection

1. In what ways was this exercise difficult?

_____

2. What were the barriers to accurate observation?

_____

3. What can you do to improve your ability to observe accurately?

_____

Case Example: Assessing the Context of Evaluation

Objective

To learn to assess the feasibility and likelihood of successful agency evaluations

Case Example

You are one of fifteen social workers who conduct groups in your foster care agency. Your director, Carlos, asked you to evaluate the effectiveness of the group component of the program. There are several types of groups that your agency provides. The most popular are support groups for foster parents. In these groups, workers help foster parents learn to cope with challenges. Your agency provides services to the Latino and the Southeast Asian communities. The majority of the foster parents in your program are white. About half of the caseworkers do not have formal education in social work but are members of Latino and Southeast Asian communities. The other half are white social workers with BSW and MSW degrees.

Carlos informed you that you will be given a release of 10 percent of your time to conduct the evaluation. He said that you will have a total budget of $500. Carlos made it clear that he chose you for the job since your enthusiasm, openness to growth, and education will be helpful in conducting an evaluation. As you have only been with the agency for a year, he let you in on some of the history of evaluations at the agency. Five years ago, researchers from a local university were contracted to provide an evaluation of the program. Many of the workers were resistant to the evaluation process. The researchers implemented many changes in the documentation process specifically for the evaluation. Workers felt unduly burdened by the changes. Each week, group leaders were required to complete an assessment of all their clients' progress toward their five most important goals. The researchers became frustrated with the workers' noncompliance. When they finished the evaluation, they provided a report that most of the workers found offensive. Some of the workers said that the researchers did not pay attention to cultural issues, citing their heavy-handed criticisms of the late start of some of the groups. Carlos wants you to figure out a way of conducting an evaluation that does not upset the staff. He is under pressure from upper administration to prove the impact of services. He does say, however, that you will have his total support in completing the project. He asks you to think about the project and come back to him in a couple of days to discuss your involvement.

Writing and Reflection

Use these questions as a guide to help you decide what you would want to discuss with Carlos about taking on the project.

1. What are the most significant barriers to the successful completion of this project?

_____

2. How will you discuss the project with your coworkers?

_____

3. How might clients be involved in the process?

_____

4. What skills can you use to help the other workers become invested in the evaluation project?

_____

5. How can you deal with the resistance in a way that will help the evaluation process?

_____

6. What are some methods for making the evaluation process as unobtrusive as possible?

_____

7. How might this project affect clients?

_____

8. Are the resources provided (time and money) sufficient for completing the project? If not, how might you obtain additional resources?

_____

9. After reviewing your answers to the preceding questions, develop a plan of action.

_____

Assessment of Group Dynamics

Objective

To develop your ability to assess group dynamics

In-Class Exercise

Group leaders frequently do not spend enough time assessing group dynamics. Like assessing other aspects of groups, assessing group dynamics is not a one-time event. A good group leader constantly pays attention to the key areas of group development.

A group of five to eight students will participate in a one-session group on a topic relevant to the members of the class. It should be a topic that is intense enough for some personal investment yet does not delve into the realm of therapy (for example, students' plans for the future once they graduate is a good topic). The instructor of the course or a student shall lead the group discussion. The rest of the class will form a circle around the group for the purpose of observation.

Each student should pay attention to the four dimensions of group dynamics: communication and interaction patterns; cohesion; social control mechanisms, including norms, roles, and status; and group culture. Once the group discussion is completed, discuss as a class what each person observed.

Writing and Reflection

1. What were your general impressions of this group?

   _____

2. What did the leader do well?

   _____

3. What would you have done differently if you had been the leader?

   _____

4. What group dynamics seemed to be helpful to the group process?

   _____

5. What group dynamics seemed to detract from the group process?

   _____

6. Describe the various roles of the different group members.

   _____

7. Based upon your initial assessment, what would you do with this group if it met for subsequent sessions?

   _____

Scanning

Objective

To develop your ability to pay attention to the individual members and the group simultaneously

Scanning is a group skill that is as important as it is difficult to master. When one scans, one simultaneously pays attention to the group member who is speaking as well as the rest of the group members. Scanning is a vital skill. If group leaders focus only on an individual and not the group as a whole, they will soon find that they are the center of attention, and all communication will soon go through them. Failure to scan often leads to low levels of group member participation.

In-Class Exercise

Break into groups of five. There should be an additional person for each group. This person will serve as an observer/consultant. Members will take turns being the group leader. For five to ten minutes, the group leader will practice scanning while group members conduct a discussion. The goal of the exercise is for the leader to find a way of paying attention to the group member who is talking, as well as each member of the group. The consultant will gently remind the leader to scan if he or she begins to pay too much attention to individual members.

Writing and Reflection

1. What was it like to scan the group?

_____

2. In what way was it difficult?

_____

3. Discuss ways you can improve your ability to scan.

_____

Self-Anchored Do-It-Yourself Rating Scales

Objective

To develop a useful assessment tool for helping individuals in groups assess and monitor their own behavior

_____

_____

Self-anchored rating scales are useful assessment tools. These rating scales help group members monitor behaviors they are attempting to change. In order to help group members learn to develop their own scales, it is useful to practice developing them for yourself.

Self-anchored scales are appropriate when there is no standardized instrument that can be used to measure a client's condition. These do-it-yourself scales are quick and easy to use. They can be used in individual work with clients or can be used in a group setting with one client at a time or with all group members in a round-robin format. Clients are asked to rate themselves on a particular dimension (e.g., level of anger, physical pain, hopefulness, self-esteem) on a scale of 1 to 10, with 1 being not hopeful at all and 10 being the most hopeful the client could ever be. You can also use a smaller range of numbers, such as 1 to 5 or 0 to 5, but it is important to be consistent, as clients will likely remember from one week to the next what their previous ratings were. Whenever possible, ask clients to rate themselves on a dimension of a strength, rather than a weakness. For example, don't ask them to rate how hopeless they feel; ask them to rate how hopeful they feel.

In-Class Exercise

Work with a partner to develop self-anchored rating scales for each other around behaviors or feelings that you struggle with (e.g., procrastination, depression, anxiety, stress, burnout).

Writing and Reflection

1. How might such scales be useful in your own life?

   _____

2. Understanding the nature of your own resistance can help you be more empathic to the resistance of clients. What would prevent you from utilizing these scales?

   _____

Chapter 6
Ending

Group endings or terminations occur when individual members choose to leave a group (in open-ended groups), when the group comes to a prearranged ending point (in a closed group), or when the leader leaves the group. The purpose of the ending phase is to effectively transition members out of the group, helping them to recognize gains made and deal with the loss associated with the group's end (Brandler & Roman, 1999).

Regardless of the reason for ending, this final stage often elicits a wide range of intense feelings among group members and group leaders. Group members may have a sense of loss and fear as they anticipate adapting to life without the group (Brandler & Roman, 1999). Feelings of loss are often most intense when the group was a close and cohesive experience in which members shared a lot of personal information (Garvin, 1997). These feelings of loss can bring up memories and feelings associated with past loss, which can intensify the experience of ending a group.

Group endings can also be threatening to group members who feel torn between the closeness they feel to other members and protecting themselves as these relationships come to an end. Feelings of rejection, abandonment, and anger are common. For group members who have felt particularly emotionally dependent on the group, anger and depression may arise (Zastrow, 2005). In particular, for members who have had difficulties with separation in the past (in regard to romantic, family, or past group relationships), ending is likely to create stronger feelings of sadness and anger.

For other group members who have experienced great success and accomplishment from participating in the group, the ending might be bitterly sweet. They may feel sad to say goodbye but generally satisfied and ready to move on (Zastrow, 2005). For others, the ending of an intense group may be a source of relief.

Group members may respond with a wide range of behaviors and emotions as endings approach. Group leaders will see that some group members withdraw from the group, sharing less information or sitting more quietly than usual in the group. Or, in more extreme cases, group members may leave the group prematurely. In contrast, other group members may begin sharing great amounts of information and make great progress as the group comes to an end in an effort to get the most out of the group and reach their goals before the opportunity comes to an end (Brandler & Roman, 1999).

It is not uncommon for group members to regress and engage in behaviors displayed earlier in the group process. They may show up late to group or act disrespectfully toward others, rejecting established group norms. Cohesion formed during the group process may start to dissipate in preparation for these relationships ending. Group members might return to unhealthy behaviors such as negative coping methods or impulsivity. What may seem like steps backward are often reactions to the stress associated with the group ending, efforts to prove the need for the group, or anger resulting from endings that are out of the control of the group member.

Some group members may take a passive stance at the end of a group. Group members might deny that the group is ending to avoid negative feelings such as anger and sadness (Zastrow, 2005). Often members who claim that group was not important are protecting themselves from more negative emotions arising as a result of the group's ending.

Due to the many different emotional and behavioral reactions that arise around termination, group leaders should address the ending long before the final session and leave plenty of time to discuss related issues within group. While discussing termination with the group may create some anxiety for the group leader, it should never be avoided or postponed, as honest and direct discussion of termination is best for the group members.

The group leader's role is to help group members recognize that the ending of group is a new beginning, and that they have acquired many important skills and insights that they will bring with them as they move on outside the group (Brandler & Roman, 1999). The group leader should describe the types of feelings that can arise at the end of the group, normalizing the array of feelings each member may be experiencing. Group members should be encouraged to share how they are personally experiencing the group ending, and leaders should respond with empathy and acceptance of all emotions.

The group leader should also be aware of his or her own feelings about the group ending. Group leaders may feel a mixture of emotions, including sadness, guilt, and ambivalence. When comfortable, the group leader should choose to genuinely share some of his or her own emotions about the group ending, using modeling to demonstrate that these emotions are normal and sharing them is important. Outside of group, leaders should self-reflect regarding their responses to members' reactions to the group ending, trying not to take negative reactions personally (Northen & Kurland, 2001). Especially in cases where the leader is leaving the group, he or she should discuss members' feelings about his or her departure openly, clearly explain reasons for leaving (e.g., promotion, transition to new role, personal reasons), and be aware of his or her own feelings of guilt and loss as the group is transitioned to a new leader (Zastrow, 2005).

In addition to processing emotions, the ending of group should include evaluation of the success of the group and the progress individual members have made.

Reflection on the group process can be done in structured activities. For example, the group leader might have the group draw a large time line of the group process, noting important points in the group process, highlights, difficult obstacles, the development of group cohesion, and the group's formation. This often involves reminiscing about experiences the group has had together, and it leaves group members with a sense of all that has been accomplished in the group.

Honest reflection should bring up discussion of goals for further improvement and work still to be done. This is a chance to talk about the future and identify ways that members will follow through with continued growth after the group ends. At this point, the group leader should encourage group members to seek support informally from other people in their lives or seek formal services as a replacement for the support they received in group.

Exercises
Ending Group Meetings

Objective
To gain awareness of the issues involved in ending a session

Writing and Reflection

1. What are the most important issues pertaining to ending a group meeting?

   _____

2. How would ending a task group and a treatment group differ?

   _____

3. What issues must you pay attention to when you are ending groups with different ethnic and racial populations?

   _____

4. What skills do you need to improve to be more effective at ending group meetings?

   _____

Understanding Behavior in the Context of Group Stages

Objective
To develop an understanding of how the stage of group life affects members' behavior

_____

_____

Since many of the behaviors of group leadership are predicated on the stage of development of the group, it is important to understand the various stages of group development, and what is normative during each stage. In the beginning stages, most groups are concerned with planning, organizing, and establishing cohesion and positive norms. During the middle phases, the group should be focused on its main work, whether this is the completion of a specific task or growth and support. The ending stage should be characterized by the completion and evaluation of group efforts. This may entail completing tasks or dealing with separation.

Reflection and Writing

List examples of behavior that may run counter to the normative group behavior for each stage. How might these behaviors negatively affect the functioning of a group?

1. Beginning stage

_____

2. Middle stage

_____

3. Ending stage

_____

Class Discussion

Discuss the issues that each class member came up with. How would you deal with these problems if you encountered them in task or treatment groups?

_____

_____

Workers' Feelings Regarding Termination

Objective

To develop insight into how you respond to ending, termination, and loss

_____

_____

Workers must be able to help members through the often difficult termination period of a group. For many clients, group experiences are profoundly meaningful sources of change and growth. For some, group membership may represent the first time they have felt truly accepted and validated in their lives. Therefore, being able to handle the emotional reactions of group members is crucial for group leaders. Also, termination reminds people of generalized losses in their lives and can trigger unresolved grief reactions.

Group leaders often have issues of their own around the topic of termination. We all bring experiences from our pasts into the group. Group workers are not immune. Group workers must be conscious of how their own emotional and behavioral styles concerning endings affect group members.

Writing and Reflection

1. What is the hardest part of endings for you?

_____

2. How do you typically deal with endings?

_____

3. What about your style of dealing with endings do you think is valuable?

_____

4. Are there any aspects of your style of dealing with termination that you would like to change? If so, what are they?

_____

5. How might you go about changing these behaviors?

_____

Writing and Reflection

The following questions pertain to more general considerations about endings and terminations of group.

1. What are the most important considerations in terminating a treatment group?

_____

2. What are some ways of helping members to continue their interpersonal growth and learning after the group has ended?

_____

3. What negative consequences might there be if members do not fully process the ending of the group?

_____

4. How would you handle a group member who has been dropping hints during the past few sessions that the ending of the group is a painful experience but expresses only positive feelings during the closing session?

_____

5. The treatment group you are conducting is holding a follow-up session a couple of months after the end of treatment. What sort of planning should be undertaken for this group?

Giving and Receiving Parting Gifts

Objective

To develop skills in terminating groups

This group activity is designed for use in ending a group with clients, but it can also be used to commemorate the ending of an academic course in group work. Detailed here is a protocol for use with clients.

At the last group meeting, it is important to discuss issues related to termination and let each member express to the others what roles they have played in his or her improvement of functioning. This exercise can be used to recognize the departure of one or several members from the group while others continue on.

The facilitator distributes a three-by-five card for each group member in the group. Everyone is asked to write on the card their "gift," or wish, for that person, either realistic or idealistic. Group facilitators should also participate in giving and receiving the gifts. Index cards are then collected and redistributed, and each person receives a card with a gift from each member and the leader, too. In a round-robin fashion, each member reads his or her gifts out loud. Examples of gifts that we have seen given at the end of group membership are "new knees that don't hurt you so much," "a boyfriend who loves you just the way you are," "the courage to quit your job," "a lot of forgiveness that you can give to your parents," "a mirror so you can see how the world sees you," "all new friends so you can get rid of the ones you have," "modesty," and "the ability to see clearly what you have done to your children." While many gifts will likely be positive and affirming and capture the members' strengths, some of the most helpful gifts are those that confront inconsistencies and blind spots that were exposed during the course of group work.

Class Discussion

1. Why does the protocol recommend that the group leader participate in giving and receiving parting gifts?

---

2. Those gifts that confront inconsistencies and blind spots are often the most helpful. Examine why this is.

_____

3. What gifts would you like to give to those closest to you in your life?

_____

Case Example: Ending Group Meetings

Objective

To learn how to assess group endings

Case Example

Charles is a clinical social worker at an inpatient drug and alcohol treatment center in a veterans' hospital. For the past twenty weeks, he has conducted a therapy group with eight veterans. The purpose of the group has been to help the men come to grips with the issues that have led to their use of drugs and alcohol. A key goal of the program is to help men work through the social issues that act as triggers to substance use. The group is very mixed in terms of ages and ethnicity. Two of the men are African American, one is Asian American, and another is half Latino. Three of the men are Gulf War veterans, and the rest are older Vietnam vets. This is the first time two of the men have been in treatment; the others each have been in treatment at least once before.

The start of the group was very difficult. Group members were resistant or reluctant for different reasons. Many of the men had learned in their lives and in the service that "real" men do not discuss their feelings in front of others, and that to do so is a sign of weakness. A young man of Chinese descent learned from his family of origin and his culture that to discuss one's problems was to bring shame to the family. During the early sessions of the group, Charles did a good job of addressing these issues. He recognized that some of the men may not always be comfortable talking about their feelings and at times would prefer to be action oriented. Charles conducted exercises that focused on behavioral change and validated discussion of affect when members of the group raised the subject. Over time, the men became comfortable with each other and began to discuss their feelings as well as their thoughts and behaviors in more intimate detail. Three weeks before the group is to end, Charles brings up the topic of termination. He tells the group that it is typical for people to have a hard time when things end, especially with experiences where people have gotten to know each other well. Realizing that the men may be reluctant to explore these difficult feelings on a group level, he asks them to spend a few minutes writing about how they typically leave situations. He tells the group that it is his pattern to minimize endings, stating that he casually tells others that he will see them later. He lets them know that he had to work hard at not minimizing endings, since this was his natural pattern. After the group members have written for about ten minutes, he asks the men to share what they wrote in dyads. After the men talk in their dyads, he asks the group members to share with the group as a whole what they discussed, if they are comfortable.

Writing and Reflection

1. What skills did the group leader exhibit?

2. Do you agree with the timing of the leader's discussion of endings? Write about your reasons for agreeing or disagreeing.

3. What was the most effective intervention?

4. What would you have done differently?

5. What would be some intervention options for the last half of this meeting?

6. How would you address the issue of endings during the next two sessions?

Chapter 7
Skills Groups

Purpose

The primary purpose of a skills group is to help group members develop techniques and skills to address some problem or issue in their lives. This is often accomplished using a combination of teaching skills and behavioral components to demonstrate and practice skill use. Skills groups target a variety of different issues and may be used preventatively when people transition to a new stage in life (e.g., study skills groups for new college students) or reactively when people are coping with a difficult problem (e.g., anger management groups for domestic violence perpetrators). Skills groups have been shown to be helpful in building skills related to physical health, social development, and academic success (Brigman & Campbell, 2003; DeRosier, 2004; Salmon, Ball, Hume, Booth, & Crawford, 2008).

Stress management groups are a popular form of skills group. In these groups, members first learn how to recognize their stress levels and identify stress triggers in order to increase awareness of when stress management skills are needed. They then learn and practice techniques for decreasing stress, such as imagery that involves replacing stressful states with images of relaxing situations to reduce physical reactions to stress. Physical strategies such as deep breathing and muscle relaxation are often taught in conjunction with imagery (Zastrow, 2005). In addition, skills for recognizing negative/irrational thoughts (such as exaggerating the magnitude of stress or minimizing one's ability to handle the stress) are often taught so that group members can then learn to question whether these thoughts are realistic and replace them with positive thoughts about their abilities to cope with stress. In this way, group members learn cognitive and behavioral skills for stress reduction.

Groups for time management are especially helpful for people who are transitioning to demanding job or school roles. Time management groups often begin by helping members evaluate how they currently spend their time and then teaching members how to prioritize tasks, make the most of their time, organize themselves, and practice managing their time on a small scale (for the next day or next week). Group members might also learn how to say no to projects and how to overcome procrastination (Zastrow, 2005).

Skills groups have also been developed to increase social skills. These social skills groups, often targeting children who do not get along with their peers or who are new to school, aim to improve listening skills, observation skills, and communication skills. Children learn how to compromise with others, make new friends, appropriately self-disclose, empathize with others, and find common ground with peers and then practice these skills. Such groups have been shown to increase children's self-esteem and decrease their social anxiety (DeRosier, 2004). For adults, social skills groups can prepare group members to benefit from other forms of groups. For example, members who want to join a support group or want to learn job skills would benefit from learning the social skills necessary to successfully interact with peers or employers. Specialized social skills groups have been developed for children and adults with autism, a disability that makes social interactions challenging. Skills groups teach autistic children to greet others and play with peers (Barry, Klinger, Lee, Palardy, Gilmore, & Bodin, 2003), and adult groups show promise in helping members develop conversation skills (Howlin & Yates, 1999).

A final example of a skills group is the anger management group. These groups often target people who have identified problems handling their anger, often coming into contact with the law because they've acted aggressively in public or toward their spouses. Anger management groups involve identifying situations where anger appears to get out of control and developing techniques to use in these situations. Group members practice pausing before reacting to their emotions, deep breathing, relaxation, and using positive self-talk, such as "I can handle this situation in a nonviolent way." In addition, anger management groups teach communication skills and methods for being assertive rather than aggressive (Williams & Williams, 1994). These groups may include involuntary members; as a result, group leaders spend considerable time developing members' motivation to change by discussing the negative consequences of anger that is not controlled.

Structure

As you can see from the examples above, skills groups often begin by helping members identify and understand the problem that will be addressed. Group members are successful in groups to the degree that they can identify specifically how the problem affects their lives and moments when the problem seems most severe for them personally. After members have begun to understand the problem, group leaders teach skills to address the problem. Skills are often modeled by the group leader or shown in videos to give group members a sense of what using each skill looks like. Finally, group members practice using the skills both within group and outside the group in real-life settings.

Group members spend a great amount of time in skills groups practicing the skills they learn. Group members usually demonstrate skills using role-playing. During role-playing, the group leader may coach the group members, offering suggestions for improving the way they are using the skill. In addition, after role-playing or modeling by the leader, group leaders give feedback. A review of what is difficult about implementing certain skills and methods members have used to master those skills may follow.

Role of Leaders

Skills groups often involve a curriculum that is structured and directed by the group leader. Consequently, group leaders spend a lot of time preparing for group, putting together lessons to teach skills as well as activities to help members practice implementing skills learned. Skills learned in group should be specific and practical so that group members are able to utilize them outside the group. To accomplish such specificity and practicality, group leaders should establish an overarching goal or aim for the group, which can then be broken down into several short-term objectives. For example, if the overarching aim is getting a job, specific goals may include how to search for a job, how to put together application materials, and how to interview. In most skill groups, group leaders serve as teachers, facilitators of discussion, and models.

Role of Members

Members of skills groups are most successful when they are open to learning new ways of thinking and behaving. Not only must they be open to the idea of change, but they must be willing to actively work toward developing skills through practice in group and outside the group. Sometimes role-playing in group can be uncomfortable for group members who are learning new skills. Group leaders and group members can work to create an atmosphere of acceptance and withhold judgment by recognizing that all group members are learning these skills for the first time and that their ability to use skills will increase with time and practice. Furthermore, when members give feedback to one another regarding their demonstration of skills, it is important that they comment on both the things their fellow group members do well and the things they can improve.

Exercises

Use of Therapeutic Silence

Objective

To learn how to use silence in groups

Silence can be used in interpersonal communication to convey a variety of messages, from empathy to lack of concern. Knowing how to skillfully use "therapeutic silence" in group settings is a skill to be developed. In a 2003 survey of studies, Hill and Thompson discovered that silence in therapeutic relationships is useful in accomplishing the following: facilitating reflection, encouraging responses, facilitating open expression of feelings, providing time for problem solving, and giving clients time to think about what they want to say. These periods of therapeutic silence can last from as short a time as three seconds to as long as several minutes or more. The more confident a group worker becomes, the more comfortable he or she is allowing the group to be silent.

In-Class Exercise

1. Separate into small groups. Talk for about five minutes about a problem one of the group members is experiencing. When there is a break in the conversation, rather than jumping in and saying something, allow for at least one minute of silence to pass. What did you think about during that minute? Ask the other group members what they thought about. Do you see any benefit in allowing this pause, rather than continuing with the discussion?

_____

2. With your group, discuss when using silence would be helpful to group process and when it would convey the wrong message.

_____

3. Are there certain client populations that would be better suited to the use of silence than others?

_____

4. As a group leader, what can you do to allow a group to experience therapeutic silence when there is a monopolizer in the group? Would it be appropriate to impose silence by saying, for example, "Now we, as a group, are going to take two minutes to silently reflect on all that was discussed today. Afterward, we will go around and ask everyone to summarize their gains today in a word or phrase. We'll start now"?

_____

Confronting Blocks to Effective Communication

Objective

To improve communication through the use of "I" messages

_____

_____

"I" messages are a type of verbal sentence structure that increases the effectiveness of communication by reducing the message receiver's defensiveness. Some clients are prone to using "You" messages and aren't even aware of it.

The use of "I" messages in place of more accusatory "You" messages is a helpful skill to develop toward effective communication. An example of an "I" message is "I feel neglected when you go out with friends every Friday and Saturday night because I get lonely waiting up for you. I wish you would save a weekend night for me each week." An example of a "You" message is "You wreck my weekends and are so rude to me. You obviously like your friends more than me!"

While most instruction around the use of "I" messages can take place in an individual setting or in a didactic lecture setting, the following exercise encourages the use of effective communication in a group setting. For further reading on this topic, visit http://www.drnadig.com/feelings.htm.

In-Class Exercise

This group activity is a lighthearted way to confront a serious unhealthy communication pattern. A buzzer is placed in the middle of the group, where everyone can reach it. Group members are invited to press the buzzer if they hear someone in the group state his or her perceptions using "You" language. Members can even buzz themselves. This activity is helpful for confronting barriers to healthy communication in an atmosphere of group support. An added benefit is that it teaches all group members to be cognizant of effectively phrased statements in others, and this experience can carry over into their own lives. Clearly, this activity cannot be utilized during an entire group session or it might impede healthy sharing. Also, it is not appropriate for use with people who have very maladaptive patterns of communication or personality disorders or are hypersensitive to public correction. This group activity has been used successfully in groups focusing on divorce recovery issues, women's self-esteem building, and depression, and in groups with adult children of alcoholics. It is likely to be successful in similar skills groups.

Stimulating Indirect Discussion of Difficult Topics

Objective

To continue to work on communication skills

In-Class Exercise

This technique is designed to stimulate group discussion of members' perspectives in an indirect way that protects their privacy. This group activity, which allows group members to talk about issues that they would not ordinarily discuss in front of others, is adapted from one presented by Sheafor et al. (1994). Group participants are given several three-by-five cards. On each card is written the start of a sentence probing for sensitive information, such as "Before a hitting episode, I feel . . . ," "When the caseworker brings up the topic of foster care, I feel . . . ," "When I can't afford food, I . . . ," and "When I am around my relatives' children, I feel. . . ." Participants complete the sentences and place the index cards back into a pile without indicating their names on the cards. The group leader shuffles the responses and reads them aloud and invites discussion of each response. The goal is that each person indirectly receives either appropriate support for his or her answer from the group or appropriate confrontation about a maladaptive response. The end result is that group participants are able to challenge the faulty belief that no one feels the way they do.

Try this activity in small groups in your classroom. The instructor or a group leader can prepare prompting sentences that are relevant to your coursework or academic program but are sensitive in nature. Examples include "I believe this program does not have a representative amount of racial diversity because . . . ," "The mistake I am most afraid of making after graduation is . . . ," and "I am afraid to admit in class that I believe. . . ."

Reflection and Writing

1. What did you write on your cards?

   _____

2. What did you learn that you had in common with your classmates that you were unaware of before this exercise?

   _____

3. What sentence do you wish had been written?

   _____

Chapter 8
Support Groups

Purpose

Support groups, also called mutual aid groups, involve group members coming together to give and receive help around a common goal. These groups are usually voluntary and address social or personal issues (Zastrow, 2005). Support groups may be created to help group members transition through difficult life experiences, such as immigrating to a new country or coping with a recent divorce. Alternatively, support groups may also be used to provide support in dealing with a specific problem. For example, Alcoholics Anonymous groups help members maintain their sobriety, and grief groups provide support for parents who have lost children.

As discussed in previous chapters, identifying a common purpose or goal at the beginning of the group is essential to the success of the group. This common purpose binds members together and moves problem solving beyond helping each individual to helping the group as a whole (Gitterman & Shulman, 2005). Consequently, support groups, like others, should start with a phase in which the purpose and expectations of the group are openly discussed and agreed upon. In contrast to other types of groups, where the group purpose is often suggested to the group by the social worker, it is especially important in support groups that group members voice their individual expectations and hopes for the group and that a consensus is reached.

A primary aspect of support groups is shared empathy. Because all group members share a common experience or problem, they are in a position to truly understand what the others are feeling. Participating in a group in which others have had similar experiences allows members to encourage one another to share personal information while also challenging one another to make changes. In addition, support groups are used to normalize the experiences of group members. In doing so, members feel less isolated while developing positive relationships with others (Gitterman, 2006).

Empathizing often leads to mutual problem solving in support groups. Group members can share personal stories of coping and resilience with other members. In sharing these experiences, the group can help individual members problem solve and develop plans of action to deal with the issues they are facing. Group members help each other by admitting to their shared problems and calling on each other in moments of crisis (for example, if an addict has an urge to use, he or she may rely on the group to cope with these urges). Other members who have had similar experiences can then offer advice based on their previous successes.

As group members offer their experiences and support to one another, the benefit is mutual. Giving help is rewarding, and reviewing past successes while recognizing challenges that have been overcome builds confidence and motivation for the helper (Steinberg, 2004). This mutuality encourages a cohesive "all-in-this-together" mentality, and group members get the sense that being a part of the group is mutually rewarding.

Structure

Often support groups take place in a circle so that members can meet face to face with other members. A social worker in a support group would likely sit as a member of the group or sit peripheral to the group structure. Because the purpose of the group is for members to support one another, the leader would most likely not sit at the head of the group, as in other more directive groups, such as psychoeducational and skills groups.

In some cases, such as some AA groups, members may sit facing forward and those who need support may move to the front of the room to share their thoughts or feelings. This is one particular structure for support groups that provides a platform for members to be heard without involving much discussion among group members.

Role of Leaders

The social worker takes a less directive, more peripheral role in the support group than in other types of groups. The social worker may help welcome members to the group and provide a general starting and ending point, but the bulk of the work is initiated and directed by the group members. Rather than providing information or teaching new skills, the social worker facilitates dialogue that is mutually beneficial for members. If a support group focuses on coping with an alcoholic spouse, for example, the social worker may introduce a topic such as relapse and ask open-ended questions regarding group members' experiences with their partners' relapses. The worker might encourage members to share their experiences, both positive and negative. As members share, the leader may take a more passive role and let members learn from and support one another.

The leader's primary role is to help the group overcome barriers to mutual aid (Shulman, 2009). To do this, the group leader seeks to increase openness, honesty, trust, and empathy among group members. These building blocks allow group members to rely on one another and motivate them to engage in the change process as a cohesive group. In beginning a support group, the social worker might explicitly state that members will have ownership of the group and play active roles in directing conversation and sharing information. Members are bound to have differing perspectives during the group process, and the social worker should encourage debate among group members while setting norms for respectful disagreement.

Role of Members

Group members are expected to actively share information and provide support during the group. The information shared may be in the form of knowledge, past experiences, feelings, or reactions to others, but the support group relies on the expectation that all members are willing to actively participate and share during the group (Steinberg, 2004). Such an active role requires members to disclose both their struggles and their successes. Sometimes active participation means providing support in the form of a listening ear that empathetically understands other members' feelings related to a certain problem. In addition, members may challenge each other to view problems from a new perspective or to overcome barriers that are preventing them from reaching their goals. In this way, support means more than a shoulder to cry on but also involves calling each other on irrational thoughts or poor choices (Gitterman, 2006). Group members should be honest about their perspectives and should openly disagree with other members if they hold differing points of view. This can be difficult for members who are accustomed to avoiding conflict, but it is vital to engaging in genuine interactions that lead to change (Steinberg, 2004).

Exercises

Identification of Feelings

Objective

To learn to identify and manage emotions

_____

_____

See http://www.psychpage.com/learning/library/assess/feelings.html for an excellent list of feelings words.

The first step to working on healthy ways of managing the expression of one's feelings is learning to identify those feelings. Often people have difficulty putting names to their emotions, as it necessitates a level of introspection that is not often required of people. Also, having multiple feelings at once can confuse a person. For example, a mother watches her young child run into the street with cars driving by. She yells at him, saying, "Don't you dare go in the street again or you'll be in serious trouble!" What is she feeling? It is likely that she is feeling a multitude of emotions at once, such as fear, love, anger, relief, and helplessness. If asked, she might have difficulty putting a name to these feelings. Feeling more than one way at once, especially opposite feelings such as love and hate, is called ambivalence.

Using a group activity of asking group members to identify their current feelings in round-robin fashion is a helpful way of teaching this skill. Group leaders should model the use of feeling words by routinely mentioning how they feel about or have felt about various relevant issues.

In-Class Exercise

1. Conduct a feelings identification round-robin in class.
2. Consider the following scenarios. Identify possible feelings each person may be experiencing. Can you see opportunities for feelings of ambivalence?

   - A woman is in the hospital recuperating from a serious traffic accident. Her husband, from whom she is currently separated, arrives to visit her in the hospital.

     _____

   - A single mother helps her son pack for college.

     _____

   - A sixteen-year-old boy gets his driver's license and is about to take his parents' car for an errand.

     _____

   - A man is about to be released from prison after serving a seventeen-year sentence for a rape he committed.

     _____

   - A man is about to be released from prison after serving a seventeen-year sentence for a rape he did not commit.

     _____

   - An undocumented Mexican immigrant crosses the border into El Paso. She is about to give birth and needs medical help.

     _____

Exploring Strengths: Mining for Hidden Strengths

Objective

To develop your ability to identify strengths in group members as a means of helping them overcome difficulties

_____

_____

Since members of treatment groups usually join to get help resolving specific problems, it is easy for group leaders to become overly focused on problems or deficits. However, a key principle of social work practice is that individuals are often able to overcome their problems and difficulties when they are helped to maximize their internal and external strengths and resources.

In-Class Exercise

Conduct an interview of a classmate. The purpose of the interview is to discover as many of your classmate's strengths as possible. During the interview, you will want to look for general strengths, as well as strengths related to culture. Try to find as many positive things about the person as you can. Explore how your classmate has used each of these strengths to fulfill his or her dreams and face challenges.

Writing and Reflection

1. What did you learn about the person you interviewed that you might not have discovered if you had focused solely on his or her problems or issues?

   _____

2. How was the tone or quality of this interview different from that of interviews you have conducted in the past?

   _____

3. How have the person's strengths helped him or her overcome the dilemmas in his or her life?

   _____

4. What strengths from the person's culture and cultural experience did you discover?

   _____

5. How might group work be different if the leader focused on strengths rather than problems or weaknesses?

   _____

6. How might this exercise affect your group work practice?

   _____

7. What skills does one need in order to work from a strengths perspective?

   _____

Chapter 9
Treatment Groups

Purpose

Treatment groups aim to help group members gain insight into problems and develop strategies for change. Often members of treatment groups struggle with more serious emotional issues or problems than the members of other types of groups (Zastrow, 2005). Group members find treatment groups to be a safe environment in which to work toward changing thoughts, feelings, and behaviors, thus leading to goal achievement and improved functioning. Treatment groups have been shown to be particularly effective in treating a variety of mental health and substance use problems, such as depression, anxiety, post-traumatic stress disorder, and co-occurring disorders (Garcia, 2004; Hendrickson, Schmal, & Ekleberry, 2004; Mueser et al., 2007).

Treatment groups often take place in outpatient clinics, hospital settings, and private therapy settings. This type of group often plays a critical role in transitioning individuals out of more intensive hospital settings by providing a place to connect to others with similar issues in an outpatient setting. In doing so, group leaders can help members work through problems while also monitoring their symptom levels to maintain functioning and avoid rehospitalization. Agencies often encourage therapeutic group work not only for the benefit of the clients but also because it is cost effective to have one social worker help a number of clients simultaneously.

Structure

A variety of different therapeutic approaches are utilized in group formats, such as reality, transactional, client-centered, cognitive-behavioral, and solution-focused therapies. The structure of a treatment group often depends, in part, on the therapeutic approach guiding the work. For example, let's say a woman joins a treatment group because she needs to become more assertive in her communication with others, particularly her partner and her coworkers. A behavior-oriented group might have this group member visualize being assertive in certain situations and then role-play assertive interactions in front of the group to get feedback. A transactional analysis group, on the other hand, might address the same problem by analyzing the internal games the individual plays in her interactions with others, naming those games, and recognizing the negative consequences of those games in order to decrease those types of interactions. Leaders choose a therapeutic approach to guide their group work based on a variety of factors, including the evidence regarding which methods are shown to be most effective for specific problems, the leader's training and comfort using different approaches, and the type of approach endorsed by the agency.

Regardless of the therapeutic approach guiding the group work, most treatment groups take place in a circle and include no more than eight members to ensure that all participants are given ample time to discuss their thoughts, feelings, and experiences. In the first few sessions of the typical treatment group, members explore their problems as a group. Members discuss when their problems began; the severity of their problems; and methods they have been using, successfully and unsuccessfully, to address the problem. As the group sessions progress, the group should begin moving toward problem solving and spend time exploring solutions as a group (Zastrow, 2005). Confidentiality is critical in treatment groups, as members share sensitive and private information. Accordingly, all members should be asked to sign confidentiality agreements stating that they will not discuss personal information or stories shared within group.

Role of Leaders

Treatment group leaders are likely to take a very active role in group. Treatment groups are most similar to individual therapy sessions but take place in a group format. Rather than simply allowing members to talk, group leaders should approach treatment groups with a clear idea of what creates change in people's lives and a collection of techniques or tools to facilitate that change. Running a treatment group requires knowledge, skills, and practice in the therapeutic approaches to be used, as well as knowledge of interviewing skills and group dynamics.

In addition, leaders must feel comfortable engaging group members at a deep level. For example, group members are likely to feel intense emotions during treatment groups, and the group leader is responsible for creating an atmosphere that is open and safe in order to encourage this type of sharing and analysis. Often treatment groups can become intense, and ending the session can be challenging. The group leader is responsible for keeping the group on schedule even when the discussion becomes very intense. When the time is up, the leader must signal the group to wrap up its session. Giving a summary of the group's discussion and having each member share a personal goal to achieve before the next session are both helpful ways to transition members out of group.

Role of Members

Participating in treatment groups allows members to both receive help and offer help to others. The depth and degree of change expected in treatment groups requires members to genuinely commit to the group and the work and challenge it may involve. While content discussed in group may be similar to content in individual counseling sessions, the benefit of treatment groups is that members can observe others working through their problems, offer empathy and suggestions to fellow group members, and receive feedback not only from the therapist, but also from the group members. Helping others allows members to view their own issues in a different light and gives members a sense of value that is rewarding. Zastrow (2005) stresses that group members and leaders in treatment groups should be offering empathy (attempting to understand each other's feelings and thoughts by identifying with them) rather than providing sympathy or pity to group members struggling with issues in group. In addition, group members are in ideal positions to help each other deal with relational issues. When fellow members are working on relationship and interaction skills, such as becoming more honest or direct in their communication with others, they can use the group as a place to practice new skills and receive feedback.

Exercises
Implementing Plans

Objective

To practice implementing a plan for a treatment group, thereby practicing the process of converting plans into action

In-Class Exercise

Below is a plan written for a treatment group for stress. For this assignment, six to eight students will act as the members of a treatment group for stress, and the rest of the class will serve as observers. Either the instructor or a student may serve as the group leader and will enact the group plan for dealing with stress. The members of the group should not role-play but will be asked to be honest about what life events are causing them stress. If a student serves as the group leader, he or she should be given a week to prepare for leading the group.

Round-robin (five minutes): Names of members and current level of stress from 1 to 10

Mini-lecture (five minutes): The causes of stress

Dyads (ten minutes): Discussion of personal stresses

Group discussion (ten to fifteen minutes): Process dyads, focusing on commonalities and solutions

Class (fifteen minutes, time permitting): Teach relaxation method

Class (five minutes): Process and end

Class Discussion

After the exercise, discuss in class what worked well and potential areas for improvements, both in terms of the leader's behavior and the plan.

Writing and Reflection

Create your own plan for a stress group. What would you do differently? Write out your plan, put it away for a day, and then critique it. By not critiquing your plan right away, you will give yourself space to be more objective.

Treatment Group Case Example

Objective

To assess group interventions with children and youths

Case Example

Sally is a social worker for Children's Care Society, an agency that provides residential treatment services to children and adolescents in community-based group homes. Most of the children and teens who have been placed in the homes have emotional or behavioral problems that have proved to be too challenging for their parents to manage or are children in the foster care system who cannot be maintained safely in traditional foster care. Sally is responsible for individual, group, and family therapy for five houses of adolescent girls. The group homes use a milieu treatment approach, whereby paraprofessional residential treatment counselors implement treatment plans that Sally develops. Sally holds group sessions with each group of children twice a week. Groups vary in size, depending upon the number of residents in each house. The groups are open ended, yet many of the clients live in the home for six to twelve months. At times there is fluctuation in membership, as clients occasionally are hospitalized, run away, or are discharged to a more or less restrictive setting.

One house of girls has recently started to get out of control. The two girls who have a history of acting-out behavior have involved several of the six other girls in leaving without permission, coming home late, and possibly drinking and using drugs. The two girls are currently at risk of being placed in a more restrictive setting far from the city. During a recent session, Sally started a conversation about an event that happened the previous night. Four of the girls left the group home after dinner and did not return until three in the morning. Sally stated that the purpose of the group for that day would be to help the girls look at their behavior and see what the potential consequences would be, and to help them make choices. Joan and Kim, the two girls who were the primary leaders, both said that they did not have to talk about anything that they did not want to talk about, since Sally had told the group that they could set the agenda. Expressing empathy, Sally answered that there was merit to their argument, that the group was for them, and that they certainly could not be made to discuss anything they did not want to talk about. Sally also explained that the situation in the group home had escalated to a point that if changes did not occur, it was likely that they would be placed in more secure settings and would be given far fewer choices in the near future. Sally suggested that she would like to help prevent this from happening, and that she hoped the girls would make choices now that would preserve their right to make choices in the future. Sally said that it was impossible for her to make them stay in the group, and that it was merely her job to help them reach their goals. Sally pointed out to Kim that she had the stated goal of being a singer, and to Joan that she wanted to become a veterinarian. She posed a question to the group: "How are your current choices going to affect your future goals?" Two of the girls who were followers of Kim and Joan began to discuss their fears about the future and worried how their behaviors might be affecting their lives. One discussed how her friends had told her that she was starting to change, and that this bothered her.

Writing and Reflection

1. What might the worker do at this point to help Kim and Joan?

2. Which of the five social work roles might be useful for Sally to take at this point? Describe different roles that might be of value.

3. What kind of resistance and reluctance might arise at this point, and how might Sally deal with it?

4. What type of planning might Sally do for the next session?

5. What type of activities or exercises might be useful?

Handling Reluctance and Resistance in Treatment Groups

Objective

To learn how to deal with reluctant and resistant clients by practicing validating their feelings

Many clients come to group reluctant to participate. Some clients are mandated by the legal system, feel coerced by other service providers, or come to treatment to save relationships. Regardless of the degree of their resistance, workers must validate clients' often mixed feelings about participating in groups.

Additionally, workers should try to uncover feelings and thoughts that underlie their behavior. Often, resistance can serve as a means of self-protection.

In-Class Exercise

In pairs, practice responding to the following behaviors or statements.

1. A nineteen-year-old Puerto Rican client is mandated to drug and alcohol treatment as part of his sentence for dealing drugs. The client states, "I am only here 'cause my PO [probation officer] told me I have to come, but nobody can make me change anything."

_____

2. In a group for battered women, a thirty-two-year-old woman tells the group that she is not going to talk about what her husband did to her. She says, "I am here to listen and learn how to live my life, but I am not going to talk about what has happened to me."

_____

3. An eight-year-old in a play therapy group for hyperactive boys sits with his arms crossed during the first three sessions and does not say anything.

_____

4. A sixty-five-year-old man in a support group for new residents of an assisted living situation states, "I don't believe in this group therapy stuff. It will not make me healthy again, and it will not bring back my wife. What do you think you can really do for me?"

_____

Writing and Reflection

Since dealing with resistant and reluctant clients is often difficult, it is important to explore your feelings about working with reluctant and resistant clients, and your responses to them.

1. What is the most difficult thing about working with resistant and reluctant clients?

_____

2. What are your biggest fears about working with reluctant clients?

_____

3. In your responses to the scenarios above, what did you do well?

_____

4. In your responses to the scenarios above, what would you like to have done differently?

_____

Treatment Group Case Example

Objective

To begin to develop skills in culturally competent group practice

Case Example

Sue is a social worker who is also a paid staff member of a small program serving GLBT members of the community. The purpose of the program is to help GLBT people meet their social needs and to provide them with support. Sue runs several support groups for different constituents, as well as a therapy group. The therapy group is for depressed GLBT youths. The group is viewed as an adjunct to other forms of treatment, as most of the clients are also seeing Sue or other clinicians for individual therapy. Several of the clients are also taking antidepressants. The members of the group see it as a valuable aid in overcoming their depression. Few mental health service providers in the very conservative community in which they live have much experience with openly GLBT people. During one recent session, Adam said that he was becoming increasingly depressed. Sue checked to see if he was thinking about or planning on hurting himself. He stated that he was not thinking of harming himself but was feeling life was hopeless. Adam is a junior at a local college and recently came out to his parents. His parents, who are extremely conservative and members of a sect of a faith that views homosexuality as a sin, did not respond well. They kicked him out of the house and told him not to contact them as long as he engages "in that lifestyle." Adam had been very close to his parents, and their rejection led him to question his value as a person. Adam wondered if his parents were right. He began to believe that he was indeed going to go to hell. He reasoned that since he could not deny his homosexuality and thus would always be separated from his family, he would live in hell and go to hell when he died. He became increasingly distant from old friends who accepted his homosexuality, as well as new friends in the GLBT community. Adam reported feeling different from many people in the group, since he is Mexican American and the other members are white. Other members of the group related to Adam. The leader asked the group if anyone would like to respond to Adam. Several expressed empathy and shared that while their situations might be different, each one of them felt a degree of isolation and shame that was affecting their lives and leading them to become depressed. Many of them also wondered out loud if they would ever feel less depressed and wondered if treatment would ever help.

Writing and Reflection

1. What cultural factors must the worker consider when developing treatment plans for members of this group?

2. What environmental interventions might be used to decrease the sense of isolation of the group members?

_____

3. What within-group interventions might the worker use to decrease the isolation of group members?

_____

4. What strategies might the worker use to change the depression Adam is feeling as a result of his beliefs, thoughts, and feelings?

_____

5. Develop a plan for a middle session for this group.

_____

6. Analyze the plan for potential problem areas.

_____

7. What other interventions might also be used to ameliorate some of the group members' depression?

_____

The Empty Chair

Objective

To learn to use creative props in group work

_____

_____

Made popular by Gestalt therapist Fritz Perls, the empty chair technique helps clients understand their feelings toward themselves and others. Used to help clarify interpersonal conflicts, it helps a client see the issue from every angle. This method is often used in individual work with clients but can also be used in a group setting where the other group members can give support and also gain through vicarious learning, where they see their peer receive insight that they can also use in resolving their own interpersonal conflicts.

First, with the group member's permission, the leader places an empty chair in the center of the group or in front of the member of focus. The chair represents the person or problem the client is facing. This could be an estranged parent, an ex-spouse, the sum total of all men who have victimized a person, an elusive job, or one's own cancer or other illness. The client is then asked to speak to the chair, explaining his or her feelings and perceptions. Then the client is asked to get up and sit in the empty chair and respond to what he or she just said, from the perspective of the other person or the situation. After this, the client goes back to his or her chair, and anyone in the group who wishes to is invited to sit in the chair and respond with any supportive comments he or she may have. As group members have success with this technique, more hesitant or resistant group members will be more willing to try it.

A modification of the empty chair technique called the dual chair technique, in which the empty chair represents a part of the person, can be used with especially insightful group members to clarify intrapersonal conflicts. Examples of intrapersonal conflicts are values dilemmas, seemingly inconsistent patterns, procrastination preventing people from reaching goals, and the repetition of self-defeating patterns in relationships or decision making. For instance, a young woman who always finds men to date in rowdy singles bars and then finds it insulting and offensive when they are interested in a sexual relationship could play out both of these roles using the dual chair technique. In one chair is the side of the young woman that enjoys the wild bar scene. In the other chair is the side of the woman that desires to have other dynamics of a romantic relationship emphasized before the sexual elements. The side in one chair can ask the other why she repeatedly visits those places when they yield hurtful experiences for her. The other chair can ask why she is so turned off by sexual attention when she appears to desire it. With the leader's help and the group's support, she can work toward finding the root causes of her choices. The last step is always to make sure the client "collects all parts" of himself or herself and feels reintegrated. Clearly, this exercise is not suitable for mentally ill or severely personality disordered clients. Clients can be reassured that a short exercise like this one will not cause them to develop dissociative disorder or multiple personalities.

Confronting Faulty Self-Talk

Objective

To learn to use some cognitive-behavioral techniques in group work

---

The term *self-talk* refers to the messages that we give to ourselves. One of the underpinnings of cognitive-behavioral therapy is confronting self-talk that is faulty. A first step in this process is for clients to begin to identify when and in what way they experience faulty self-talk. In this exercise, group leaders present group members with examples of four different categories of faulty self-talk. Group members are then asked to brainstorm what self-talk they might experience that falls in these categories. Since the exercise is phrased in hypothetical terms, clients can feel free to participate and share what their private self-talk might be. The assumption, however, is that many of the beliefs they express will indeed be true for them or at least have what Freud called "a kernel of truth."

Saying these beliefs aloud has three positive benefits for clients: (1) they can experience catharsis, or emotional release, by saying them out loud; (2) they may receive support from the group in the form of other group members saying they have felt that way also; and (3) they may let go of that faulty self-talk, since it has been identified as not based in rational thought.

The group leader introduces the topic of faulty self-talk and describes the four types of negative messages and provides an illustration for each:

1. Arbitrary inference is the process of drawing conclusions when evidence is lacking or shows the contrary to be true. For example, "The JV coach must really hate me and want me off his team, and that is why he keeps talking to me about moving me up to the varsity squad."

---

2. Overgeneralization is the process of making an overarching generalization based on only a single incident. For example, "I didn't get hired at the video store, so why apply anywhere else, because no one will want me to work for them."

---

3. Magnification is the propensity to exaggerate the significance or meaning of a single incident. For example, "My sister was late for my birthday party, so that means she doesn't care about me anymore and our relationship is doomed to end soon."

---

4. Cognitive deficiency is disregarding an important aspect or event in one's life. For example, "My father is in prison for shooting my mother because I watched too much TV."

After group members give hypothetical examples of faulty self-talk in each of these categories, the group leader can ask them to identify any of their own as a homework assignment to discuss at the next group meeting.

Chapter 10
Psychoeducational Groups

Purpose

Psychoeducational groups aim to help group members develop the knowledge and skills necessary to cope with specific issues in their lives. Of all the different types of groups, psychoeducational groups are most similar to a classroom in that the group leader has knowledge and information to share with group members who have a common interest or concern. Members of psychoeducational groups are interested in learning techniques, facts, and strategies from the leader and from each other and aim to apply this knowledge to their individual situations. In addition to developing knowledge, members also acquire skills that they can use outside the group to cope with or address problems they face.

Brown (1998) describes a process of developing self-knowledge that takes place in psychoeducational groups. This process may look similar to counseling, yet it does not require group members to delve deeply into their emotions or their pasts or to disclose extensive information about themselves (Niemann, 2002). Rather, the aim of developing self-knowledge is to examine one's situation and contextualize the information learned in group.

The types of knowledge and skills acquired during psychoeducational groups vary according to the purpose of the group. Some psychoeducational groups focus on learning to prevent problems. For example, colleges frequently offer study skills groups to freshman students. These groups teach students techniques for being successful in their new college courses by helping them make good choices about where, when, and how they will study. Similar prevention-focused groups might help high-risk youths develop safe sex practices or help struggling high school students avoid dropping out of school.

Psychoeducational groups can also focus on supporting group members during transitions in life. These groups normalize members' feelings and thoughts during times of adjustment while also teaching ways to cope with changes. For example, a social worker might run a psychoeducational group in an assisted living center for elderly clients who are transitioning from living independently to living with assisted care. These groups might inform members about common challenges that are associated with losing independence while also suggesting techniques for maintaining autonomy within the new living situation. Similar transition-oriented groups could help new parents adjust after childbirth or retirees cope with leaving their careers.

Finally, psychoeducational groups can be used to help clients learn about a particular problem or disorder they are facing. For example, young adults with a new diagnosis of bipolar disorder may go to a psychoeducational group to learn about the symptoms associated with the disorder. Learning about changes in mood, the neurobiology underlying mood changes, and methods for increasing awareness and coping with moods can be helpful to the newly diagnosed. Family members may also want to participate in psychoeducational groups, which can help them learn about the client's problem and identify ways to help their loved ones.

Underlying these different types of psychoeducational groups is a common broad goal of preparing members to make good decisions. Education often focuses on empowering clients with knowledge of their options, methods for making choices, and skills for following through with the decisions they make (Niemann, 2002).

Structure

Psychoeducational groups often look similar to a small seminar or class. Group members are likely to sit in a circle, but the leader is often positioned at the head of the group and may use visual aids to share information with group members. For example, group leaders may use a flip chart, chalkboard, or video to teach materials. Leaders also may use more experiential formats such as modeling techniques and having group members role-play the skills they are learning (Roffman, 2004). Often leaders will assign readings or homework for group members to complete between sessions. Because most of the material discussed in psychoeducational groups is predetermined (like a curriculum), the groups often occur for a set amount of time, and it is understood from the beginning when the group will terminate.

Role of Leaders

Social workers take a strong leadership role in most psychoeducational groups (Roffman, 2004). Leadership involves presenting information to group members while both normalizing their experiences and contextualizing the information to group members' specific situations. In doing so, the group leader encourages members to apply the information to their own lives. In addition, the social worker often facilitates discussions between group members regarding the material presented in group. This role involves several skills, including teaching, facilitating, and training.

Leaders often approach the group from a theoretical standpoint that guides the type of activities done in group. For example, a leader with a social learning perspective would model and role-play skills, while a leader with a behavioral perspective would help members monitor and reward behavioral skills learned in group (Furr, 2000).

Role of Members

Group members are asked to listen to and absorb information provided in group and then apply this information to their own situations. Members may want to share their own experiences and how the information provided fits or does not fit with their understanding of a topic. In psychoeducational groups, members are often joined together under one common goal. All members have sought information to better prepare themselves to deal with a common problem. This can create group cohesion and a natural group formation that keeps the group focused on its common purpose.

Psychoeducational groups are often more comfortable for clients than traditional therapeutic groups, which require deeper sharing of emotions and thoughts. People are accustomed to the format of teaching from years of attending school, so seeking help through psychoeducational groups can feel familiar and acceptable to people with a variety of cultural values and backgrounds (Roffman, 2004).

Exercises

Focus

Objective

To develop your ability to keep a group focused, while balancing the need to allow group members autonomy and self-determination

_____

_____

Group leaders must strike a balance between direction and democracy; they must avoid being overly controlling of the group's interactions yet focus group members on productive work. Jacobs et al. (2001) address several important skills pertaining to focus: establishing focus, maintaining focus, deepening focus, and shifting focus.

In-Class Exercise

In groups of four or five, take turns being the leader for ten minutes. The leader will choose a topic that he or she would like to discuss. Leaders will want to consciously practice each of the skills pertaining to focus. Each leader should make sure he or she clearly establishes the focus, maintains focus on the topic throughout, deepens the focus to a level that moves beyond superficiality, and for practice shifts the focus to another topic or ending.

Writing and Reflection

1. What behaviors did you find helpful in regard to each area of focusing?

   _____

2. What was the hardest thing to do? Why?

   _____

3. Did you feel uncomfortable shifting the focus? If so, what made this difficult?

   _____

4. Did you feel uncomfortable deepening the focus? If so, what does this mean for you?

   _____

5. Based upon this exercise, which skills would you like to improve? How can you go about making these improvements?

   _____

Life Depictions

Objective

To begin to learn methods of psychoeducational practice

_____

_____

Psychoeducational groups aim to help group members develop knowledge and skills that will be helpful for coping with specific issues in their lives. An important component is gaining knowledge about one's own life situation. Group leaders can help members with this learning through the use of three different written homework assignments aimed at increasing group members' self-knowledge. Students are encouraged to complete these assignments to gain insight into how the experience can affect a person.

Life History Grid Assignment

The first assignment is a life history grid, an example of which is presented in figure 1. A life history grid is a method of organizing and presenting data related to various periods of a client's life (Anderson & Brown, 1980). This grid is especially helpful for children and adolescents, and for adults who experienced significant life-altering events during adolescence or childhood. The identification

Figure 1 Life History Grid

Year	Age	Location	Family/Friends	School/Work	Health	Activities	Events
1994	Born 8/21	Buffalo, NY	Dad, 21 Mom, 20				
1995	1						
1996	2						Went to Disney World, don't remember
1997	3		Josh born in intensive care with spina bifida				Mom stayed at hospital.
1998	4						
1999	5			Kindergarten, JFK Elementary			
2000	6	Moved to Erie, PA	Lost best friend, Henry	First grade, Mill Grove Elementary	I had an operation but don't know what for		Josh died.
2001	7		Hate the kids in Erie	Second grade			
2002	8			Third grade			
2003	9			Fourth grade		Played baseball	I think Mom was pregnant.
2004	10			Fifth grade, Mill Grove Middle School		Played baseball	Getting Cs and Ds
2005	11			Sixth grade		Played baseball, parents missed all but one game	Parents went to China to try to adopt baby.
2006	12			Seventh grade		Tried out for football, cut from squad	Dad and Mom separated. Dad moved back to Buffalo.
2007	13			Eighth grade, expelled	Broke fingers in a fight		Hit teacher, threatened suicide
2008	14		Girlfriend, Sarah	Ninth grade, home-schooled by mother—hate it	Depression medications		Hate myself, hate Mom, hate Dad

of life experiences at a particular stage of development can shed light on current functioning.

Genogram Assignment

The second assignment is to draw a family tree, only going a step further and adding data on individuals and relationships, such as addictions, personality traits, and broken or enmeshed relationships. The clinical term for this is a genogram, but for the purpose of a homework assignment for group members, the term *family tree* is more appropriate. After the assignment is complete, ask members to reflect on what they have drawn and whether they see patterns of addictions, unhealthy relationships, broken relationships, and so on. The group leader might want to encourage participation in this assignment by giving each member a large piece of paper such as butcher paper, poster board, or extra-large copy paper to use for the family tree.

Eco-map Assignment

The third assignment is for each group member to draw his or her social and community network. The social work term for this depiction is *eco-map*. Ask them to map out their friends, family, religious organization and other group memberships, work or school, and neighbors, and the resources they access in the community. When group members bring these to the next group meeting, other members can benefit from seeing how other members may be more engaged in their community. Those who are isolated may gain ideas about how to "plug in" and get more engaged. Ask members if anyone included this group on their social and community network. Those who have complicated and crowded depictions may realize from the group's feedback that they need to streamline their lives and that the "crowded" nature of their life situations may be a source of stress.

Writing and Reflection

1. Which of the three assignments did you enjoy the most? Find most challenging? Learn the most from?

_____

2. What new insights did you gain from each of the three life depictions?

_____

3. What types of clients do you think could benefit most from these assignments? Why?

_____

Chapter 11
Task Groups

Purpose

The primary purpose of task groups is to complete some predetermined goal or accomplish some action. You may find that you have participated in a task group without calling it by that name. Social workers are likely to encounter many task groups throughout their careers through their employment and participation in different agencies and organizations. Such organizations are governed by a board of directors (one form of task group), who are tasked to run the organization (Zastrow, 2005). Organizations also involve committees established to complete certain tasks, such as a hiring committee or a budget committee. In addition, social workers meet regularly with colleagues in staff meetings created to make decisions on agency policies and procedures as a group.

Social workers meet regularly in task groups with other professionals to discuss specific cases and make team decisions on how to best serve their clients. For example, an adolescent who is breaking the law may warrant a case staffing (one form of task group) that involves meeting with his or her teacher, school social worker, child protection worker, psychiatrist, parent, and probation officer to accomplish the task of reducing the child's problem behaviors. In groups comprising people from different professional backgrounds, communication can be challenging. Social workers and other professionals might be surprised by the amount of jargon used in these meetings. In task groups, special effort should be made to use language that everyone in the group understands as well as to describe objectives and strategies in language familiar to consumers and community members (Fernandez, 1997).

While task groups may seem more business oriented and less intimate than other types of groups such as treatment groups and support groups, relationships in task groups are still important. Members find task groups that involve close interpersonal relationships, friendships, and team unity among members to be most successful (Hirokawa, Degooyer, & Valde, 2000). Having positive relationships with other members allows people to understand where others are coming from and identify each other's strengths and weaknesses, which allows the group to run more smoothly and effectively (Hirokawa et al., 2000).

Structure

Task groups are larger than most other types of groups. They usually take place in meeting or conference rooms, and there is usually a clearly designated leader or chairperson who runs the group. A written agenda is often used to organize the group meeting and review goals, and one member is usually assigned to take group minutes so that each session can begin with a brief summary of decisions made at the previous meeting. Task groups usually last about one hour (no more than two hours) to ensure that members stay engaged and productive.

Groups begin by identifying a clear set of objectives that will help them achieve the overarching task at hand. The group then develops a list of strategies for reaching each objective, being specific about what the desired outcome will be (how the group will know when it has reached its goal), and what the time frame is for achieving each objective.

The group should be very clear about who will be responsible for each action step. The group should try to divide work evenly and make sure that all members have responsibilities. Group members will feel more cohesion if they are actively involved in the task group and are making individual contributions (Fernandez, 1997).

In deciding on action steps, the task group may use brainstorming to discuss a wide range of options and opinions. When group members perceive open communication in the group (i.e., they feel their voices are heard, that they can have an open discussion, and that all members are valuable and contribute equally), they feel the group is more successful in accomplishing its task (Hirokawa et al., 2000). Once ideas are on the table, the group can then narrow down options and make decisions regarding the best course of action.

Often task groups do not reach a complete consensus, in which every member agrees on one course of action. The group should decide how it will reach a consensus when members disagree. Often task groups vote on decisions, making choices based on what the majority of the group believes. However, groups may decide that a large percentage of the group (75 percent, for example) must agree to determine a solution. Other groups give ultimate decision-making power to the group leader or to a select group of three or four people, who have final say in situations where the larger group is split on an issue. These options should always be discussed early on in the group process so that members are clear on how consensus will be reached, including a discussion of how members want to voice their opinions (e.g., by silent vote, hand raising, orally).

In attempts to reach a consensus in task groups, conflict will naturally arise. Group members are likely to, at some point, have differing opinions on an issue. Often these differing opinions can be useful. Groups in which everyone agrees all the time lack critical thinking and may fail to come up with the best solution to a problem. Conflicts should be discussed openly, and each person should be given a chance to voice his or her opinion and ideas so that the group may make an informed decision. Only when conflicts become unprofessional or go on for a very long period of time and the discussion no longer seems productive should a group leader step in to end the discussion, change topics, or try to reach a conclusion.

Role of Leaders

A strong leader is needed to keep a task group focused. The group leader runs meetings and moves the group toward developing clear action strategies. Sometimes discussions lead to conversations about unrelated material, and the leader is responsible for bringing the discussion back to the original topic or keeping the group on task. In addition to being directive and structuring the time, the group leader also uses his or her facilitation and counseling skills to encourage discussion in group by asking open-ended questions and paraphrasing others' points in order to join everyone in the group toward a common goal (Fernandez, 1997).

Group leaders should be comfortable with conflict, which may arise in group; give everyone a chance to voice their opinions; and be assertive if conflicts become personal or unproductive. The group members rely on the group leader to set norms regarding how they interact with one another. They want to feel that they have a chance to contribute but also be assured that they have a strong leader guiding the process.

It is important to keep a task force moving. This means that there is constant action toward accomplishing its goals. Groups can lose momentum when they do not meet regularly enough, when conflict results in a standoff with no resolution, or when action steps are not clearly defined or assigned. A sense of movement creates the energy necessary for the group to achieve its aims (Douglas & Machin, 2004).

Role of Members

Group members bring different expertise and knowledge to task groups. Their primary role is to contribute to accomplishing the task at hand. This includes developing clear objectives and action strategies to reach those objectives, and carrying out those strategies.

Group members should be involved to the greatest extent possible in establishing the rules and goals of the group. They should also contribute their ideas regarding specific action strategies the group should take to accomplish its overarching task. The more involved each member is in the group, the more invested in its success he or she is likely to be. The assignment of titles that reflect members' responsibilities (e.g., treasurer) is a form of recognition that can increase their feelings of status and responsibility and has been shown to result in higher group member satisfaction and improved performance (Lucas, 1999).

Exercises

Brainstorming

Objective

To practice and develop skills in facilitating brainstorming

_____

_____

Brainstorming is one of the most important methods of helping various types of task groups develop creative ideas and means of problem solving. During brainstorming, energy is focused on creative thinking and generating ideas, not upon the evaluation of these ideas. Brainstorming thus helps groups think outside the box.

In-Class Exercise

Divide into groups and practice brainstorming. One person will serve as the leader during the exercise. The exercise can be repeated more than once so several students may lead. Suggested brainstorming topics are ways of improving your school of social work, ways of developing healthy friendships, things in the community that need to be improved, or problems with welfare reform. Remember the four rules for brainstorming: (1) freewheeling is welcome; (2) participants should not engage in criticism; (3) quantity is wanted; and (4) combining, rearranging, and improving ideas is encouraged. The leader should pay special attention to helping the group generate ideas, not evaluating them.

Writing and Reflection

1. What went well during the brainstorming exercise?

_____

2. What would you do differently next time?

_____

3. What do you perceive to be the value of using this technique?

_____

Focus Groups

Objective

To learn how to conduct a focus group

_____

_____

Focus groups are a wonderful way of collecting in-depth data about community needs, perceptions of agency functioning, and many other topics of interest in indirect or macro social work practice.

In-Class Exercise

A team of two students is asked to volunteer to be the leader of a task group. They can conduct a focus group on any topic that might be appropriate to your school of social work. They will prepare to conduct a task group the following week. They will make sure to plan a specific agenda, discuss methods for recruiting and screening students from the class, and think through methods of facilitating the group.

Writing and Reflection

It is now your turn to analyze the data.

1. What generalizations can be made from the data?

   _____

2. What can be learned from exceptions to patterns in the data?

   _____

3. What would your recommendations be, based upon the data?

   _____

Task Group Skill Assessment

Objective

To learn how to facilitate the assessment of group members' skills in task groups

_____

_____

In task groups, it is important to help individual members assess what they can contribute to the group. Since empowering individuals to take ownership for their assigned tasks is essential to successful task group facilitation, it is often useful to help individual group members assess their strengths related to the task.

In-Class Exercise

In groups of five to eight, students will be asked to be members of the first session of a task group. The purpose of the group is to assess the resources in your community. In this exercise, the group leader will facilitate a group in which the members assess their own skills in regard to the task. The leader will then help the group members discuss their strengths in regard to completing the task. It is important that the leader spend time drawing out and validating the strengths of the members. Members of task groups often have more skills and resources than they are aware of.

Writing and Reflection

1. How well do you feel the group members assessed their own strengths?

_____

2. What factors seem to lead to accurate self-assessment?

_____

3. What might be the advantages of having group members assess their strengths and choose actions based upon these strengths, versus having the leader assign tasks?

_____

Task Group Case Example

Objective

To develop task group skills

Case Example

Jose is an eighteen-year-old who is involved in a conflict between himself, the school he attends, his wraparound social worker, and the school district administration. Jose was referred for wraparound services (community-based mental health services that provide treatment in the home, school, or community) to help him succeed in his urban high school in the northeastern part of the United States. Jose started attending his school within the last few months. Prior to this, he lived in a residential treatment facility that had a self-contained school. Jose lived in residential treatment facilities for over six years. His mother, who raised him by herself, placed him due to his aggressive and often violent behavior. While in residential treatment, Jose was able to decrease the incidence of his aggressive behavior dramatically, although at times he was still aggressive toward peers and adults. He also carries the diagnosis of mild developmental delay.

When Jose turned eighteen, he left his placement and returned to the community. He found an inexpensive room near where his mother lived. Jose decided that he wanted to attend the local high school. Although he had not attended public school in over five years, he stated that he felt tired of going to "dummy schools" (private schools for children with developmental disabilities and partial hospitals). Still mandated to provide educational services for Jose, the school district placed him at the local high school in a special education class designed for students who are mildly intellectually disabled. While Jose is very happy being in the community high school, he is not happy with being placed in this class.

Although he recognizes that he has "learning problems," he does not want to be in a class with adolescents who are mentally retarded, all of whom are lower functioning than himself.

After two weeks in class, Jose became verbally aggressive with the teacher's assistant and other teens. The school personnel began to see Jose not only as mentally retarded, but as having serious emotional and behavioral problems as well. They have started to believe that Jose is inappropriate for their school. Jose, on the other hand, sees his aggression as a function of his placement in a classroom that is not to his liking. School personnel told him not to come back to school until he had a one-on-one wraparound worker with him for the entire school day. School personnel saw this as an intermediate step until a more appropriate school setting could be found by the school district administration.

A community team consisting of Jose, his mother and his aunt, school personnel, a representative of the school district, and the wraparound social worker met to discuss the problem.

The conflict can be succinctly stated as follows. Jose is in conflict with the school, as he wants to return to school immediately and does not want a one-on-one wraparound worker with him full time. The school district does not want to pay for an approved private school placement and thus is not in conflict with Jose, but with the school personnel. The district recognizes that in sending Jose home for two weeks, the school violated his rights and made them susceptible to litigation. School personnel do not want him back in school at all, but certainly not without full-time intensive support. The wraparound social worker is in conflict with the school, as his agency, and the funding source, would be willing to provide half-day services but questions the need for full-time interventions. Also, the social worker recognizes that it is the school's responsibility to provide an appropriate educational program for Jose, and that while wraparound services can help Jose deal with his emotional and behavioral problems, it is the school and school district's responsibility to meet his educational needs.

Writing and Reflection

1. What strategies would you use in the group to help negotiate a resolution to the conflict?

_____

2. What potential difficulties do you see arising during this group?

_____

3. What are some tasks that might be assigned to different group members in order to help resolve this situation?

_____

4. What between-group tasks might the group leader do?

_____

5. How would you evaluate the effectiveness of this group?

_____

Dealing with Conflict

Objective

To increase your ability to tolerate the inevitable conflict that occurs in groups

_____

_____

Conflict is a nearly inevitable part of group work. In task groups, leaders must learn how to manage conflicts in order for tasks to be completed. Many people are uncomfortable dealing with conflict.

In-Class Exercise

This in-class exercise may also be done independently. The following questions may be answered and reflected upon regarding your general reaction to conflict. Break into groups of five or six. You will simulate a task group meeting in which there is a fair amount of conflict. In this exercise, the leader will not intervene but should merely witness the conflict. It is important to note that normally, leaders must find ways of intervening during many conflicts. Take turns being the leader, and tolerate conflict for five minutes.

Writing and Reflection

1. Describe what was most difficult for you about being present during the group conflict.

_____

2. What methods did you use to tolerate the conflict?

_____

3. What can you do to increase your ability to tolerate conflict in the future?

_____

Responding to Conflict

Objective

To increase your ability to manage conflict

In-Class Exercise

Remaining in the groups used in the previous exercise, take turns leading a task group in which there is conflict. This time, the leader will intervene to ensure that the group manages its conflicts.

Writing and Reflection

1. What skills did you use well when helping resolve the conflict?

_____

2. What was most difficult for you while you attempted to resolve the conflict?

_____

3. What might you do differently the next time a similar conflict arises?

_____

4. What skills did fellow students use that you thought were effective?

_____

Implementing Problem Solving in Task Groups

Objectives

- To learn the problem-solving approach as it is applied to task groups
- To discover the advantages and disadvantages of using task groups versus individual decision making

In-Class Exercise

The director of your school of social work has just allocated $10,000 to help students create a greater sense of community. You have been asked by the director of the department to create a process for deciding how the funds will be used. In task groups of approximately six people, develop this process. A leader will help the group apply the problem-solving approach to the issue.

Writing and Reflection

1. What worked well in this process?

_____

2. What was difficult about this process?

_____

3. How could the group have been conducted more effectively?

_____

4. What would you say are the strengths of this process?

_____

5. What are the weaknesses of this process?

_____

6. What might be the advantages of this group process over coming up with a process on your own?

_____

7. What would the disadvantages be?

_____

Task Group Case Example

Objective

To develop decision-making skills in task group leadership

Case Example

You are the director of a community-based mental health agency. The agency provides intensive social work services to at-risk children in their homes and schools. The goal of the program is to help parents and guardians, as well as teachers, maintain children with challenging behavioral and emotional problems in the least restrictive setting possible. Master's-level social workers provide individual and family therapy, and bachelor's-level workers provide one-on-one intervention for several hours a day.

The program provides a desperately needed service in the urban area that it serves. It helps reduce children's reliance on expensive inpatient and residential care. For these and other reasons, the program experienced tremendous growth during its first few years. The biggest problem the program had was hiring and training enough staff to meet its ever-increasing demand. Sometime during the third year of its life, the state contracted with managed mental health care organizations to manage mental health services in the city. At this point, things began to change rapidly for the program. Its rates were cut, and the amount of hours it was allowed to work with children decreased dramatically. Suddenly, a well-funded and solid program found itself facing new challenges and constraints. You did your best to inform the staff of potential changes. You worked with your management team to find solutions to many of the program's problems. However, staff morale began to wane. The ambiguity and uncertainty led several experienced and valued staff members to find new employment. You decided that you needed to involve staff more intimately in the decision-making processes of the program.

Writing and Reflection

Answer the following questions about how you would go about conducting the task group meetings.

1. Where would you conduct these group meetings?

   _____

2. Who should be included in the meetings?

   _____

3. How large should the group meetings be?

   _____

4. What potential conflicts might arise? How might these conflicts be dealt with?

   _____

5. How can members be involved in the decision-making process?

   _____

6. How might fact finding be facilitated?

   _____

7. What processes might be used to make effective decisions?

   _____

8. What are the potential political ramifications of these decisions?

   _____

9. How can work be monitored and evaluated?

   _____

Chapter 12
Macro Practice Groups

Purpose

The purpose of macro practice groups is to engage in larger systems change within an organization or community. Although the use of community-oriented change groups has declined in the United States over the past several decades, this is not due to their lack of importance but rather, as we have previously discussed, is the result of changing values within the social work profession. Even though individual symptoms amelioration has become the profession's primary focus, we hope that exploring macro level practices will stimulate increased interest in these practices, which are an important part of the history of social work practice in the United States, as well as a significant aspect of contemporary practice in other countries.

In other countries, macro-oriented groups are often influenced by anti-oppressive practice, the subject of chapter 13. Macro practice also consists of administrative and organizational change. The majority of groups within organizations are task groups, discussed in chapter 11. Please see those chapters for more information and exercises for developing your macro practice skills in these contexts.

One example of a community-based macro practice group exists in Colombia, South America. Colombian law mandates that mining companies must employ a social worker to serve the communities in which the mining companies operate. The social worker aids community members in negotiating with the mining company regarding issues that affect their community. The social worker meets with a representative group of community members and activists to help them navigate the complex relationship between the company and the community members, many of whom are also employees. The social worker has the difficult task of balancing community needs and the needs of her employer. Fortunately, the social worker's employment is partially protected by the federal law mandating her position. As such, she is able to view the empowerment of the community through the group process as the most important part of her role and function.

Macro-oriented groups such as this often fall under the guise of another group practice category; you will likely notice several examples throughout this book.

Structure

Macro groups may meet within many different settings and may adopt many different structures. Given that psychological and psychosocial issues are not the focus of macro groups, meetings may not always be held in private. Yet it is extremely important that members feel safe to discuss issues that are important to them. Therefore, while the temptation may be to hold group meetings in open, public spaces, group leaders should first be certain that group members are comfortable with this choice.

Role of Leaders

The role of the leader in macro groups is as a facilitator of the change process. Macro groups do not focus on intrapsychic issues. Group leaders only focus on group dynamics when they interfere with the nature of the group process. Group leaders help group members move from an individual view to a systems view of the problem or concerns being discussed. They help the group members brainstorm and evaluate potential systems-oriented solutions and then focus members' efforts on engaging in systems change. The group leader must help members develop realistic expectations for the change process and manage their frustrations if (and normally when) change does not come easily. This is a challenge for group leaders in macro-oriented groups. They must keep the group focused on the identified systems change while developing the skills and capacities of individuals (and at times helping them remove barriers), often an essential task in facilitating group aims. For these reasons, even group workers who view their work as adopting a primarily macro focus must still be well versed in helping individuals and direct practice groups.

Role of Members

The role of group members is slightly different for macro-oriented groups than it is for micro, or direct, practice groups. In direct practice groups, the primary role of the members is to focus on their own concerns and issues, and to help other group members with similar concerns. In such groups, mutual aid is the central activity. However, in macro groups, members are asked to move beyond their own personal concerns. Certainly their interest and involvement will frequently stem from how the targeted problem or issue affects their own lives, but the focus of intervention is on the system, not themselves.

Exercises
What Has Worked, What Has Not

Objective
To learn from bad examples of administrative group practice

_____

_____

Sometimes we learn a great deal not only from what others do well, but from what they do not do well. As an in-class group exercise or on your own, discuss or write about your worst experience with administrative groups and teams. Discuss what the leader did poorly and how you would do things differently. After, develop a five-point "manifesto" of what one should never do!

Building a Director's Team

Objective

Learn the value of group work for organizational leaders

Social workers frequently become administrators far more quickly than they had anticipated. As such, they can often feel unprepared for leadership positions. One unhelpful response that some new administrators have is to adopt a very isolating, "I am in charge" attitude. In other words, they overcompensate for their insecurity by attempting to seem like the boss. Often, new leaders who adopt this approach make wholesale changes without properly working with others. The results are usually poor. One antidote for this tendency is for new leaders, or experienced leaders who wish to move toward a more inclusive approach, to create a director's advisory group. This group is not an external advisory board, but a group of four or five staff who provide guidance to the director.

Using the skills you have learned so far, work in pairs to plan a director's advisory group. Develop the group for a social service program in which you are involved, or for one that you know may benefit from such a collaboration between leadership and staff. Make sure to carefully consider Jacobs's model discussed in chapter 1.

Chapter 13
Anti-Oppressive Practice Groups

Purpose

Anti-oppressive social work addresses social inequities and structural divisions within society (Dominelli, 2002). Anti-oppressive practice is not a single theoretical orientation to practice but, rather, includes various social justice, liberation, and "radical" approaches. Anti-oppressive practice is an important and influential group of theories in Canada and in some countries in Europe. Additionally, while referred to by many names, the anti-oppressive focus is very common throughout social work practice in Latin America.

Anti-oppressive groups engage in several types of change. First, they are utilized to alter real-world power differentials that exist within systems (Shera, 2003). In this sense, the purpose of anti-oppressive group work is macro-level social change of the structures that lead to classism, sexism, racism, and other forms of oppression (Razack, 1999). Second, anti-oppressive group work helps to make group members aware of and ultimately transcend the structural impact of inequality on their own lives. Paulo Freire (1970) was one of the originators of this form of anti-oppressive practice in the field of critical education. He advocated for groups that taught literacy through "conscientization," or helping members become aware of their own internalized oppression, and also taught how traditional methods of education and social structures led to their disempowerment. By becoming conscious of their own oppression, group members would begin to critically assess the sources of their own oppression, thereby becoming agents of social change themselves. Because anti-oppressive groups can focus on individuals and their own internalized oppression or on social change, they can be micro or macro in focus, or they can exhibit qualities of both. Recently, anti-oppressive approaches have focused on helping people transcend poverty, a social problem for which the micro/macro divide breaks down (Strier & Binyamin, 2010).

Structure

The structure of anti-oppressive groups is far more open than the structures of other group types, or of groups based on other theoretical orientations. This is because members of anti-oppressive groups take far more ownership for the nature of the group than do members of other group types. In general, however, anti-oppressive groups are structured to reduce or eliminate hierarchies and power differentials. Anti-oppressive groups may also find themselves oper-ating within community spaces rather than within the traditional confines of a group circle. For instance, a Theatre of the Oppressed group (an example of which is presented toward the end of this chapter) will engage in social change–oriented performances in an indoor location or even in the community. These groups are highly orchestrated and coordinated, as engagement with those who are not part of the group not only creates an opportunity for social change but also increases potential risk.

Role of Leaders

Leaders working from an anti-oppressive perspective must always be aware of the pervasive influence of power in the relationship between them and their clients (Sakamoto & Pitner, 2005). In fact, the word *client* is often not favored by anti-oppressive practitioners, who typically prefer terms such as *member*. Anti-oppressive practitioners must be continuously self-reflective about their own behavior and how they may unwittingly perpetuate power differentials between themselves and the group members. There are several important roles of leaders in such groups (Hays, Arrenondo, Gladding, & Toporek, 2010). First, they must engage and promote egalitarian relationships between themselves and members, and among the members themselves. Second, they should encourage members to participate in the decision-making processes of the group. Third, they should direct the group's focus to a critical reflection of the role that various social forces play in the development of members' problems. This is particularly important, as many group workers trained in more traditional group models will naturally focus clients on their family histories or on intra-psychic explanations of their behavior. In anti-oppressive work, the focus is on social change. Last, group leaders should help members focus on identifying opportunities to engage in individual and collective action in order to help change the structural elements of their oppression.

Role of Members

The role of members in groups that are run from an anti-oppressive perspective can be complex. In chapter 1, we explore how groups can be encouraged to move from a focus on personal problems to a critical consciousness, and ulti-mately toward social action and change. It is important to note that group members may not begin their group experience with this goal in mind; this can often be part of the theoretical/ethical perspective of the practitioner. Of course, the practitioner believes that this type of empowerment is an essential part of helping people; that through developing an awareness of the social roots of various feelings and behaviors, people can be freed from the shackles of their own personal problems. Yet, as social workers move anti-oppressive groups from an internal to an external orientation, some members might become confused about the nature of the work and therefore might come to believe that their original issues are not being addressed. Consequently, the role of the group members and the group leader must be continually negotiated.

Perhaps paradoxically, group members should have maximum ownership over the course of the group and should be increasingly empowered to take owner-ship over their own personal lives, their group, and their social environment. Agency is central to anti-oppressive approaches. Agency is a concept that derives from feminist scholarship and includes notions of empowerment, will, and self-determination. Agency also connotes the capacity to adapt to difficult and oppressive contexts such as extreme poverty and deprivation (Lindsey, 2010). Anti-oppressive practice seeks to support clients in their attempts at over-coming oppressive contexts.

Exercises

Understanding Your Own Power and Privilege

Objective

To help group members begin to understand the nature of power and privilege

---

Peggy Mcintosh (1990) notes that privilege is akin to an invisible backpack of attributes that people possess that provide them with various unearned advan-tages. This has been an important concept for anti-oppressive practices that group leaders must learn to appreciate.

In-Class Exercise

This exercise should be conducted individually, then processed and discussed in small groups. Individually, for five minutes, write about someone you know who seems to have privilege. Discuss what makes the person privileged, whether the person is aware of the privilege, and how this privilege provides him or her with unearned advantages. Now that you have applied this analysis to someone else, your task is to try to think about your own invisible privileges and advantages. Before you begin writing this phase of the exercise, close your eyes and imag-ine a very poor person of a background different from your own. Imagine this person looking at you and your life. What privileges might this person notice? How would they view your advantages?

Once members have finished, discuss this as a group. Although a group leader should be designated, he or she should take very much a facilitative role and pay careful attention to the principles explored in this chapter.

Understanding Power and Leadership

Objective

To develop an understanding of how a group leader might exhibit and use power

In anti-oppressive groups, power, and how the group leader uses it, is an essential aspect of practice. Group leaders must understand how their own attitudes and behaviors regarding power may influence the empowerment of group members and the group overall. Answer the following questions and discuss them in class. Given that issues around power are sometimes difficult to discuss, we recommend using dyads rather than larger formats in order to encourage disclosure and feelings of safety.

Writing, Reflection, and Discussion

1. When do you know that you are feeling the need to be in control?

2. Describe when you are comfortable giving away power and when you feel the need to maintain it.

3. Do you worry that a group might get out of control if you share power and control with group members? Please explore this.

4. What have you learned thus far that might conflict with the type of leadership needed for an anti-oppressive approach to practice? How might this influence your behavior as a group leader?

5. What are the situations in your life where you have felt powerless? Have these made you more or less likely to feel the need to be in control or have power in groups?

Enacting Oppression: Adapted from Theatre of the Oppressed

Objective

Develop skills in an expressive approach to anti-oppressive practice

One of the most powerful ways of understanding oppression is to observe it. Additionally, although it might be easy to *say* how one would intervene in social situations in which oppression occurs, it is far more powerful to engage in in-vivo, real-life interventions. This exercise is adapted from Augusto Boal's Theatre of the Oppressed (1993). Theatre of the Oppressed was originally developed by Brazilian theater producer and radical educational theorist Augusto Boal. A close associate of Freire, Boal saw the possibility of a theater designed to liberate people from oppression. Boal sought to transform the oppressive relationship between the oppressed and the oppressors through exploration of personal experiences (Dennis, 2009).

In the Forum Theater, the lines between actors and the audience, who are called "spectactors," are largely eliminated. During Forum Theater's enactments, the actors play out scenarios in which various types of social oppression occur. The spectators can ask for a scene to be stopped when they witness incidences of oppression, and they can suggest interventions to the actors or engage in the intervention themselves.

In-Class or Group Exercise

With a small group, plan a skit that characterizes an example of a social oppression. Act out the skit for the remaining group members, inviting them to make suggestions for how to intervene and deal with the oppression or even to become involved in the intervention themselves. After the skit is completed, discuss the various interventions as a full group. Below are a few questions to guide your discussions.

1. What inhibits people from suggesting interventions?

   _____

2. What are the risks involved in engaging in the suggested interventions?

   _____

3. What interventions were effective and why?

   _____

Chapter 14
Eating Disorder Groups

Eating disorders involve extreme eating behaviors, such as rigid restriction of food, gorging on large amounts of food, purging after eating, and obsessing over food intake. Types of eating disorders include anorexia (severe food restriction or starvation to keep oneself unhealthily thin, often accompanied by an intense fear of weight gain and distorted body image), bulimia (bingeing on food and then purging through vomiting, exercise, fasting, or laxatives in an out-of-control cycle), and binge eating disorder (uncontrolled overeating during short periods of time) (Koch, Dotson, & Troast, 1997). Disordered behaviors are often related to self-criticism and perfectionism or other painful underlying emotions such as anger, sadness, fear, shame, and powerlessness. The disordered behavior is used to cope with this underlying pain and gives the person a sense of control.

Group treatment for eating disorders can take place in a number of settings, including outpatient, residential (in a specialty unit or facility), and inpatient settings, depending on the severity of the symptoms and group members' physical and psychological health. Regardless of the setting, leaders of eating disorder groups should work closely with other professionals connected to group members' treatment, including nutritionists, physicians, psychiatrists, and nurses. These professionals can conduct thorough assessments and monitor members' physical health. In addition, group leaders should be aware of the increased risk of other mental health problems associated with an eating disorder diagnosis, including depression, anxiety, phobias, and substance abuse problems (Koch et al., 1997). Some of these symptoms may be addressed within the group; however, concurrent treatment may be needed, including medication for related disorders.

Eating disorder groups should be small (five to eight members) and include members with similar disordered eating symptoms (Hall, 1985). While group treatment often works well for bulimics and binge eaters, special care should be taken with anorexics, as they are often more withdrawn, anxious, rigid, self-focused, and competitive until they reach a healthy body weight. Individual treatment may be more effective until they can focus on others, be more flexible, and share experiences in group (Hall, 1985).

Eating disorder groups should address both the symptoms of the eating disorder (e.g., rigid thinking, restricting food intake, bingeing, purging) and the underlying problems leading to the eating disorder, including psychological, relational, and societal factors (Koch et al., 1997). Often, as symptoms and disordered eating behaviors are addressed and diminish, other underlying emotions arise in group. When this happens, emotions should be recognized and normalized, and the group should be used to practice healthy ways of exploring and expressing painful emotions. To do so, group leaders can use one of several different types of groups or a combination of group types to help group members, including treatment groups, psychoeducational groups, skills groups, and support groups.

When a therapeutic approach is taken, cognitive-behavioral therapy is often utilized, especially if the eating disorder has been short term or has not yet reached serious levels. This model is often used with bulimic group members and members coping with binge eating disorders (Anorexia Nervosa and Related Eating Disorders, 2005). Cognitive-behavioral therapy involves identifying irrational thoughts about food and weight, making connections between those thoughts and one's feelings and behaviors, and actively working on changing thoughts and associated behaviors. In contrast, insight-oriented therapeutic groups focus on helping members identify and talk about the problems underlying their eating disorders, such as poor self-esteem and emotional pain. Group therapy can also be especially helpful for learning to manage relationships, as interpersonal relationships may play a role in the lives of group members with eating disorders (Birchall, 1999).

Psychoeducational groups help members dispel myths about eating and food, learn about nutrition and health, and develop their own healthy eating plans. Members gain knowledge about their bodies and the effect their behaviors have on their health. In addition, psychoeducational groups can help individual members map out time lines of their eating disorders and understand and identify when their eating disorders began, emotions and experiences that contributed to the disorder, how it has progressed, and where each member would like it to go in the future (Koch et al., 1997).

A skills group approach to eating disorders helps group members develop and practice techniques for coping with stress and underlying emotions, thereby avoiding disordered eating behaviors. These groups might involve members documenting their eating disordered behaviors to increase their awareness and then learning and practicing replacement behaviors that decrease stress in a more constructive manner.

Because group members struggling with eating disorders often feel isolated and alone, support groups can play an important role in recovery. Often, however, support is one component of treatment and is supplemented by other psychoeducational and therapeutic components. Support groups can be helpful to the extent that they incorporate information regarding the consequences of disordered eating, include an overall aim to achieve and maintain a healthy body weight, are supportive and inclusive, and involve members who are actively working to normalize their eating behaviors. While support can help members feel less ashamed and better connected with others, group leaders should strongly discourage members from sharing information about techniques for losing weight such as dieting and purging behaviors.

Exercises

Interpersonal Intervention: Applications to Self

Objective

To work through a structured process of change and become more familiar with implementing change

_____

_____

It is far easier to guide group members through a change process if you have worked through one yourself. When a client comments that change is hard and might not be possible, being intimately aware of the dynamics of working through change will help you address them in a less hypothetical or detached, clinical manner. This is not to say that you must self-disclose what issues you have worked on in your own life, but working on change ourselves usually leads to a greater level of authenticity. Having worked through the process yourself, you will be able to remember what the steps felt like and will have an easier time helping people through their resistance to change.

Writing and Reflection

Pick one problem area that you would like to change. The questions below will guide you through the four steps of interpersonal change.

1. Describe the nature of the problem.

_____

2. Identify thoughts, feelings, and actions that are associated with this problem.

_____

3. Describe the connections between specific thoughts, feelings, and behaviors.

_____

4. Analyze the rationality of your thoughts and beliefs. How accurate are they? Do they help you in your life?

_____

5. With what would you like to replace the behavior you are attempting to change?

_____

6. Write down thoughts and beliefs that support your new behavior.

_____

7. Develop a plan for following through on making the change.

_____

Releasing Our Shame

Objective

To help group members work on resolving their shame

_____

_____

There is an expression that we are "only as sick as our secrets." As we know from working with clients, when they express things that they are ashamed of and receive acceptance and validation, they are able to face their demons and make changes. The same is true for our prejudices. Expressing them to a safe person can help reduce our shame and the impact of these beliefs. As Martin Luther King said, "The truth shall set you free."

With a person who you feel is safe, discuss your answers to the questions in the previous exercise. If this is done as an in-class exercise, make sure that all participants know that their job is to listen, support, and accept. This is also a good exercise for practicing empathic listening.

Writing and Reflection

1. What did you learn from this experience?

_____

2. In what way might this change your beliefs or behavior?

_____

3. What other beliefs do you need to let go of?

_____

Family Sculpting

Objective

To learn techniques for responding to family issues

_____

_____

This group technique can be used with group members who are experiencing any kind of problem with a root in their family dynamic. Since clients with eating disorders often have difficulties with interpersonal relationships and family relationships, this group activity is especially suited to this type of group.

Family sculpting is designed to help a client, during a group session, reenact and relive important aspects of his or her family's behavior. The client can choose to enact the family of origin, or, if the client is older and has his or her own children, he or she can enact that current family system. *Sculpting* is an artistic analogy that is used to describe how the client physically arranges or molds the family in a way that conveys meaning, much like a sculptor working with clay (Sheafor et al., 1994).

Small groups in your class can participate in this exercise, to give you an idea of what it feels like to participate as the sculptor or as an enactor. First, the group leader introduces the concepts by explaining, "We are going to try something a little different today. I need a volunteer who is interested in gaining some insight about how she fits into her family at home. We are all going to get up out of our chairs and help with this. What I need is for someone, without talking, to arrange group members into a picture of what his or her family looks like. For example, you could choose someone to be your father, who is remote and disinterested. That person would be standing outside our circle of chairs with his back to us and arms folded. Your teenage sister, whom you see as the baby of the family, might be sitting on your mother's lap. And maybe your older sister could be trying to block your access to another group member who represents food and binge behaviors. And you will play yourself, showing us what role you play in the system of your family. Now, who wants to volunteer to go first?" With each subsequent volunteer, the process will require less coaching on the part of the group leader, and insights may get deeper as clients become more comfortable with the process.

After the family has been sculpted, the group leader will ask the group to look around and study the dynamics portrayed. Then group members return to their seats, and the leader asks everyone to discuss their own feelings and perceptions.

In-Class Exercise

Try this activity in your classroom groups. What role did you play? How did this role feel? What insights did you gain?

_____

_____

Chapter 15
Groups with Persistently Mentally Ill Adults

Persistent mental illnesses include psychiatric disabilities that result in serious impairment in social functioning and lead to either hospitalization for long periods of time or frequent re-hospitalization (Garvin & Tropman, 1998). While the precise definition of persistent mental illness is often debated, the term is generally used for more serious long-term disorders, including psychotic disorders (e.g., schizophrenia), severe mood disorders (e.g., bipolar disorder, major depression), and personality disorders (e.g., borderline personality disorder) (Garvin, 2005).

Living with a persistent mental illness is associated with many challenges, including difficulties dealing with stress, keeping jobs, maintaining stable housing, and forming healthy relationships (Garvin, 2005). Furthermore, symptoms often interrupt activities of daily living, such as cooking meals, personal hygiene, and housekeeping (Gerhart, 1990). To address these challenges, groups with this client population help members develop skills, improve socialization, and cope with symptoms of their mental illnesses. Groups are provided to adults with persistent mental illness in a variety of settings, including inpatient mental hospitals when symptoms are acute or, more commonly, in community mental health centers, clubhouses, and group homes.

One common goal for persons with persistent mental illness is establishing healthy relationships with others. Mental illness can be isolating and cause clients to withdraw. Developing social skills and practicing relationship building within the safety of a group can be very helpful. Group leaders can didactically share information on communication, empathy, and listening skills and can create an environment where members can practice such skills through interactions with one another. Group leaders can incorporate social skill development into all group sessions, regardless of the topic, by pointing out positive social skills and making suggestions when negative social patterns emerge between group members.

Groups with persistently mentally ill adults also target building skills for daily living to help members increase their independent functioning. Skills groups teach methods for such tasks as ensuring personal safety in public, how to keep a clean home, job searching, medication management, developing structure, and scheduling one's daily life. In addition to talking about skills, group leaders might model or role-play how to use these skills and give members a chance to practice and/or talk about their struggles and approaches to utilizing these skills. Group members might also use imagery to visualize themselves using new skills and may use self-assessments to evaluate their ability to incorporate new skills during practice (Furr, 2000).

Coping with the symptoms of mental illness is another purpose often addressed in group. Means to improve coping methods may involve psychoeducation as well as skill development. Psychoeducational groups have been especially effective in helping people manage persistent mental illnesses (Burlingame, MacKenzie, & Strauss, 2004). For example, for group members coping with delusions, psychoeducational groups might inform members what delusions are, and skills groups might involve practicing methods for identifying, labeling, and discarding delusional thoughts (Garvin, 2005). Similarly, depressive group members can benefit from identifying depressive or self-defeating thoughts and practicing checking the reality of their perceptions.

Medication often plays a large role in group members' lives, reducing symptoms and improving functioning. Some of these medications, however, have uncomfortable side effects, and group members may dislike taking them for fear of becoming dependent. Group leaders generally need to discuss medications, their effects, and difficulties in taking them with the group, and they often need to work closely with other professionals such as psychiatrists and nurses to address this issue (Northen & Kurland, 2001).

Groups for the persistently mentally ill are often highly structured and directive (Garvin, 2005). Members often benefit from a clearly stated purpose, aim, and organization in group, and this requires group leaders to take an active leadership role. In addition, group members often have difficulty dealing with stress and instability, and this sensitivity may quickly lead to overstimulation (Rapp, 1985). Accordingly, groups are often focused on skill building and coping methods rather than insight-oriented therapy (Sands & Gellis, 2011). In fact, psychotherapeutic approaches can be ineffective or even harmful for people coping with persistent mental illness (Rapp, 1985).

Because group members are likely to cope with persistent mental illness for years, they may participate in long-term groups. Thus, engaging group members and eliciting their ongoing commitment is essential. Garvin (2005) suggests that providing refreshments, holding groups in convenient locations, and utilizing various creative formats such as games, activities, and role-playing can maintain group members' interest in the group. Groups may be conducted in an open format, so that members are able to join in for sessions when they feel they need it, rather than committing to every session for a set period of time. Furthermore, long-term group members may play special roles in the group that benefit other members and increase their own investment in group, such as introducing new members, passing out materials, or demonstrating skills.

Exercises

Five Intervention Roles

Objective

To practice each of the main intervention roles and become aware of which roles are most comfortable, and which ones need to be developed further

---

Social workers have five intervention roles that they may utilize with clients in order to help them meet their treatment goals: enabler, broker, mediator, advocate, and educator. Each of these roles represents a different set of skills that can be practiced and developed.

Writing and Reflection

To increase your insight, skill level, and comfort with each role, answer the following questions.

1. Describe your experience with each of these roles in groups and other helping situations.

   ---

2. In which of these roles do you feel most comfortable and competent? Why?

   ---

3. In which of these roles do you feel least comfortable and competent? Why?

   ---

4. What skills do you need to develop in order to become more comfortable and competent in each of the roles?

   ---

5. List and discuss three things you can do to develop these skills.

In-Class Exercise

For this activity, you should divide into groups of five. You will pick a topic that is of interest to everyone in the group. You will take turns being the leader for five minutes each. During your time as leader, your goal is to try each of these roles at least once. Group members should not be too resistant and difficult during this exercise. Due to the degree of artificiality created by attempts to switch roles so quickly, the leader may not always be as sensitive as he or she otherwise would be. After the group is over, discuss the following questions as a group or as a class, or use the questions for writing and reflection.

1. For each of the roles, identify one member of your group who performed the role well. Discuss how he or she performed the role and what skills were involved.

_____

2. Discuss any changes you would like to make as to how you performed each role.

_____

Engagement through Discussion of Current Events

Objective

To improve group facilitation skills

_____

_____

The chronically mentally ill population is well suited for skill-building groups and those focusing on coping strategies rather than insight-oriented group work. At many treatment programs that work with this population, you will find groups focusing on topics such as activities of daily living, medication compliance, and dealing with stress. Presented here is a novel idea for engaging this often difficult-to-reach population through a group discussion focusing on current events. In the past, we have successfully used this method at a day treatment center for chronically mentally ill adults.

With a group of four to twelve clients, talk for a while about some mildly controversial issues being discussed in the news on any topic ranging from politics to celebrity gossip to issues related to natural disasters or weather-related phenomena. Monitor the group for what topics seem to spark some interest or commentary from members. When a topic of interest is identified, the group leader should spend a few minutes explaining why some people feel one way about the issue and others feel differently. Then, in a round-robin fashion, go around and ask each person for his or her opinion on this issue and write the person's name and position on the board. Provide praise for every response and talk about the wisdom each person used in coming to that conclusion. After all members have been polled, look over all the comments and see how the group feels collectively. This is a good experiential exercise in empowerment, building group identity and pride, and helping this population engage in conversation that they may not be exposed to elsewhere. In our group, the clients found it so engaging that we began to copy down the results of their round-robin responses and save them as a formal record of the group's positions. Many found it empowering and verbally engaged in this group activity more than they did in activities in other skills-based groups. Examples of mildly controversial topics that might be used are banning prayer in schools, the federal government giving money to people who lost their beach homes to hurricanes, celebrities getting more famous in drug rehab, bulldozing forests to make room for families to have homes, and sending food and clothing to developing countries.

Use of Reminiscence Groups

Objective

To learn to use reminiscence techniques

Reminiscence is the act or process of recalling the past. Reminiscence groups have long been used successfully with older adults, and evidence has shown that they produce positive outcomes such as increased self-esteem, decreased depression, and improved quality of life (Soltys, Reda, & Letson, 2002). Many of these group skills and approaches for older adults can be adapted and used effectively with persistently mentally ill adults.

In a small group setting with persistently mentally ill adults, introduce the concept of reminiscence. Find out how far back group members can remember. Share some of your own early memories. Passing around a large photograph can help stir members' memories. Lead a discussion about a certain type of memory, such as cars you have owned, favorite music groups, old television shows or movies, vacation trips, and memories of the city or town as it was years ago. Be careful not to ask about topics that are likely to stimulate depressed feelings, such as dreams not pursued because of mental health issues, or relationships members have lost due to their illness. Focus on areas where the clients can find enjoyment, such as music or movies. When we have conducted this type of group with this population, the overall mood is visibly elevated, and previously disengaged group members often participate verbally and nonverbally.

Chapter 16
Elementary School Conflict Resolution Groups

Schoolchildren often experience conflict in their interactions with peers, teachers, and parents. Conflict resolution groups help children identify and understand conflict and develop skills for peacefully handling situations where conflict arises. These groups are usually conducted in school settings, either within the classroom with all students (e.g., growth/preventative groups) or in special groups for children identified to be at risk for conflict (e.g., therapeutic groups). With increased attention drawn to school violence in recent years, schools are investing more time and resources in school-based conflict resolution groups, and researchers are studying the effects of these programs. A review of the literature indicates that conflicts in schools are common, that they are often destructive, that conflict resolution groups increase students' abilities to handle conflict more effectively, and that in doing so, students have more positive outcomes, require fewer interventions from teachers, and elicit fewer disciplinary actions from administrators (Johnson & Johnson, 1996).

Conflict resolution groups teach students a number of techniques for solving interpersonal conflicts and allow them the chance to practice these strategies with their peers. Students not only learn to resolve their own conflicts but also learn to mediate conflicts between their peers (Johnson & Johnson, 2005). When children encounter situations where they disagree with someone and conflict seems likely, the group should help them express their thoughts and feelings in a nonthreatening manner, listen and empathize with the other person's perspective, develop a list of options for resolving the conflict that satisfy both parties, and decide on an option of action with the other person (Johnson & Johnson, 2005).

Accordingly, conflict resolution groups aim to build empathy, communication skills, flexibility, and problem-solving skills—traits found in students who successfully negotiate conflict situations (Lane-Garon, 2000). A key component of conflict resolution groups is increasing children's abilities to consider other people's perspectives (Lane-Garon, 2000). Those children who can correctly identify others' thoughts and emotions and understand others' points of view are less likely to become involved in negative conflict (Lane-Garon, McWhirter, & Nelson, 1997).

Specific exercises in conflict resolution groups include teaching students how to use "I" messages—statements that follow the "I feel . . . when you . . ." format.

Practicing these statements helps students express their feelings in a nonthreatening manner and identify the problem. In addition, groups may help children understand how to create win-win situations in which both parties compromise and get some of what they want. Students may also practice recognizing their responsibility and contribution to the conflict and attempt to use active listening to restate the problem from the other person's perspective. Children are generally willing to learn these types of conflict resolution skills in group and are able to use them during interactions outside the group (Stevahn, Johnson, Johnson, Oberle, & Wahl, 2000).

Elementary school children often are not able to sit still for long periods of time. They can be engaged in group through actively participating rather than only listening to information. Groups should take place in a space that has been cleared of tables and desks, where kids can sit on carpeted floor or on pillows and they have adequate room to express themselves. Activities often incorporate props or objects to symbolize the ideas taught in each session. Through the use of stories and physical demonstrations, kids can imagine and visualize interactions. Concepts can be taught and then practiced through active games, role-playing, or paired practice. Role-playing is an especially important component of building conflict resolution skills. Role-playing allows children to practice incorporating their new knowledge into action. In particular, role-playing is a critical component of training children in social skills related to conflict resolution (Santilli & Hudson, 1992). Practicing social interactions within the context of a group gives peers and group leaders a chance to offer feedback on their ability to use new skills.

After an activity, the group leader can lead a discussion of group members' reactions to the activity, including what was easy, what was hard, how it felt to practice a certain technique, and what the results seemed to be. Conflict often elicits negative emotions of fear, anxiety, stress, and sadness in many children. These emotional reactions as well as reactions to using techniques learned in group should be discussed openly in the group format (Lane, 1995). Group leaders need to facilitate discussions to help group members process their thoughts and feelings about what is done in group. While children this age are not likely to be developmentally capable of deep insights, they can talk about what they see or hear and can express, on a basic level, what they think about those events. Often the leader will recognize when a child is experiencing an emotion and can draw attention to that feeling and help the child identify that feeling in words. The use of rituals such as sitting in circles, taking attendance, and having a snack can be used to impose a structure to the group and create familiarity and comfort among group members (Lane, 1995).

Leaders of conflict resolution groups play active roles. They often function as educators, providing information to group members about what conflict looks like and methods for constructively handling it. In addition, group leaders should constantly be aware of interactions among members. In groups of elementary school children, conflicts will naturally arise, whether in the course of making decisions or working on group activities. When these conflicts arise, the group leader should use these interactions as real-life examples of conflict and opportunities to practice skills taught in group.

Recognizing the developmental abilities of children at different ages is important for group leaders working with elementary school students, as progression from kindergarten to middle school involves many great changes in development. Because different students are at different developmental stages, students' reactions to group and thus evaluations of group success may be different across grade levels. Younger children may simply describe groups as fun, while older students may be able to identify methods for peaceful conflict resolution by the end of the group (Lane, 1995). Pre-group and post-group assessments should be adapted to different age groups accordingly.

Exercises
Exploring Our Own Experiences with Conflict

Objective
To explore experiences with conflict and how these experiences influence our views about conflict and strategies for conflict resolution

_____

_____

People receive messages about conflict from a very early age. We watch our parents have conflicts; we argue or fight with friends; and later in life, we are faced with conflicts with our partners. Some people learn that conflict is negative and that one should avoid it at all costs. On the other hand, some people learn that conflict is necessary, and that one should vehemently defend oneself during conflict to prove the importance of one's perspective to others. Still others might fall somewhere in the middle, recognizing that conflict is inevitable, and sometimes productive, and that it is important to develop techniques for dealing with conflict. It is important for social work group leaders to recognize the lessons they have internalized about conflict and how it is resolved before they facilitate groups on conflict resolution.

Writing and Reflection
Take time to think about your answers to the questions below. Remembering past conflicts can be difficult, but doing so will help you identify your thoughts and feelings related to conflict and enable you to empathize with group members in conflict resolution groups.

1. Think about a conflict you've witnessed in the past. Ideally, this would be a conflict between people who were important in your life and an interaction that you remember clearly or that had an impact on you. Describe that conflict here. What was it about? How did each party respond? How did it come to an end? What messages do you think you got from witnessing this conflict?

_____

2. Now describe a recent conflict or argument that you were personally involved in. This time, pay particular attention to your reactions during the conflict. What did you do? What did you say? What was the outcome of the conflict? If you could turn back time and go back to this conflict, is there anything you would do differently?

_____

3. Describe your typical reaction to conflict. Do you run away or avoid conflict, seem to instigate conflict with others, or mediate conflict between other people? How comfortable are you asserting your point of view when you know others disagree? What techniques do you use to do so?

_____

4. Empathy is a critical component of conflict resolution. How do you feel about your ability to empathize with others? Is it easy or difficult for you to understand a situation from another person's perspective? In what contexts or with what issues is this most difficult for you?

_____

5. If you could set three goals for yourself to improve your conflict resolution skills, what would they be?

_____

Teaching Conflict Resolution Skills

Objective

To learn conflict resolution methods

In-Class Exercise

Conduct this exercise in small groups in class. Divide each group into teams of two or three people. Have the teams play against each other in a competitive card game, preferably something short (about five minutes long) that all members are familiar with, such as Go Fish. This could also be conducted using tic-tac-toe or any other short game that results in a winner and losers.

While the group plays the game, observe their interactions. How does each member make decisions about what to do during his or her turn? What happens if someone disagrees?

After the game is over, ask the winning group how they feel. They are likely to feel good about themselves and be happy with the outcome. Then ask the losing group how they feel. They may express disappointment, frustration, or regret. They may want to play again to redeem their status.

Now facilitate a discussion about the consequences of situations in which there are clear winners and losers during conflict. Might losers of conflicts feel some of the same emotions? Introduce the idea of win-win solutions to problems. Discuss how outcomes of win-win solutions might be different. Will both groups feel more satisfied? Will there be reduced incentive for continued conflict? Finally, discuss your observations of the groups during the competition. These interactions may provide examples of compromises made, problem solving, and strong versus passive leadership styles.

Writing and Reflection

1. What part of this group practice was most comfortable for you, and what part was most challenging? Think specifically about your comfort and abilities in relation to observing, instructing, facilitating discussion, asking questions, providing information, and the like.

2. What lessons and/or skills do you think group members could develop from participating in this activity?

3. In what ways would you improve this group activity to help group members better achieve these aims?

4. Discuss ways that you might adapt this group for children in a kindergarten class versus children in a fifth-grade class. What might you do differently for these two developmental age groups? What questions might you ask each group?

5. This chapter stresses the importance of helping group members understand others' points of view. Why might this be difficult for elementary school children? Think creatively about how a group leader might help children to do so. Describe an activity, lesson, or role-play that might help students understand another person's perspective, thoughts, or feelings.

6. Conflicts often arise naturally among members of conflict resolution groups. This chapter encourages group leaders to use these conflicts as real-life examples of conflict and opportunities to practice skills. How do you imagine a group leader would do this? What would it look like? How comfortable would you feel spontaneously making use of conflict that comes up in group?

_____

Chapter 17
Teen Pregnancy Groups

Although teen pregnancy rates in the United States have been declining over the past two decades, the United States still has the highest rate of teen pregnancy among Western industrialized countries (Martin, Hamilton, Sutton, Ventura, Menacker, & Kirmeyer, 2006). Teen parents face numerous challenges, including staying in school, paying bills, maintaining stable relationships, and coping with their babies' health problems (Bensussen-Walls & Saewyc, 2001; Martin et al., 2006). Teen pregnancy groups can be an ideal resource for coping with these challenges.

Teen pregnancy groups usually involve a component of skill building, psychoeducation, or support and often include a combination of these formats. Developing engaging activities is important to maintain the interest of adolescent group members. In addition to planned exercises and lessons, group leaders should ask their teen pregnancy groups what they need from group and create time to address the unique needs that arise. Leaving time during each group session for members to bring up issues and seek help in problem solving leads to group cohesion and is necessary to address the ever-changing needs of teen parents.

Groups are often composed of pregnant teens or new teen mothers, but some groups may also include the babies' fathers or the parents of the teen. Regardless of the composition of the group, these adolescents already have a lot on their plates, and special consideration should be given to making group participation convenient. Examples include providing transportation to and from group, offering healthy snacks, and making child care available during group sessions.

While pregnant teens may be coping with a variety of challenges, a few specific goals are especially important to address within group. Completing high school should be emphasized. This involves providing education on study skills, such as study habits, note taking, and test taking, as well as providing material specific to teen parents, including information on time management and balancing the demands of school and parenthood (Adolescent Pregnancy Prevention Coalition of North Carolina, 2004). In addition, how to conduct a job search, identify areas of interest, apply for jobs, and interview are all skills covered in teen parenting groups that help members achieve financial stability.

Psychoeducational groups can inform teen parents about pregnancy, giving birth, and new parenthood. Regarding nutrition, for example, the group may begin by asking members about their typical meals for one week and helping them analyze ways they can incorporate healthy foods into their meals for themselves and their babies. This includes teaching members about balanced meals, prenatal vitamins, and the connection between mother's and child's food intake.

There are a number of tasks that group members should do before the baby comes, including visiting the hospital and gathering necessary supplies, and the group can be used to list these tasks and monitor progress. Once parents give birth, addressing basic parenting skills, breast-feeding, sleep schedules, immunizations, and babies' health needs will be immensely helpful to the new parents (Adolescent Pregnancy Prevention Coalition of North Carolina, 2004).

Teens often become pregnant due to lack of knowledge or resistance to using contraceptives, and these issues should be addressed to prevent subsequent unplanned pregnancies and to decrease risk for sexually transmitted diseases (Franklin, Corcoran, & Harris, 2004). Repeat pregnancy is a risk that most teens want to avoid. Group can be used to help teens make healthy decisions about relationships and learn how to determine whether to engage in sexual activities. Often teens benefit from developing self-respect and self-esteem and making sure sex is not used to make themselves feel valuable. In addition, skill development on different forms of contraception is necessary, including how to choose a method, how to negotiate contraception use within a relationship, and how to use methods effectively. Furthermore, strategies for refusing unwanted sex should be discussed and practiced within group, as teen pregnancy has been significantly associated with sexual victimization (Boyer & Fine, 1992).

Not only do pregnant teens need to deal with financial, academic, and parenting challenges, but they also need to maintain a support system of friends and family. Pregnancy often results in isolation. Previous peer groups may move on, and if the teen is not in school, she may lose touch with good friends who seem to have different priorities. Group can offer teen parents connection to peers their age who understand what they are going through and can provide support. Furthermore, the group can help members realize they still share common interests with peers outside group and can encourage members to reach out to get together to maintain those connections. Similarly, family can offer support. Often a teen pregnancy can cause distress for the teen's parents, but involving them in group sessions to talk about the pregnancy and determine what is best for the teen and her baby may alleviate some stress and create a much needed support network.

Exercises

Assessing Problem Solving and Coping

Objective

To understand and draw connections between your own coping and your ability to assess the coping of others

---

Clients often come to groups in distress. When people are experiencing increased stress, they often do not cope as well as they normally do. It is important for group leaders to assess problem-solving skills and coping strategies that clients have used previously.

In-Class Exercise

In groups of five to eight students, a leader will assess how students cope with stress. The leader will lead a discussion by starting with the following statement: "Each of you has stated in the past that being a student can be very stressful. Sometimes we cope with stress well, and sometimes we do not. I am interested in those times when we cope with stress well. I would like us to talk about how we manage stress, specifically those times when we are doing a good job managing it. Who would like to start?"

Writing and Reflection

1. What did the leader do well?

2. What did you learn about coping?

3. What did you learn about groups from this exercise?

Writing and Reflection

Conduct an assessment of your own coping mechanisms for dealing with the stress of school. Answer the following questions in as much detail as possible.

1. What are some indicators that tell you when you are feeling stressed?

2. What changes in your life when you are feeling particularly stressed?

3. How do you relate to and treat people when you are feeling very stressed?

4. What coping mechanisms work for you when you are feeling very stressed?

5. What coping mechanisms have helped you manage your life in other circumstances (other than when you feel stressed)?

6. Do you engage in any negative coping mechanisms or bad habits to reduce stress? Describe these behaviors and their impact.

_____

7. How well are you dealing with your stress now? How does this compare to times when you are optimally handling your stress?

_____

8. Devise a treatment plan for yourself. Based upon the assessment of your coping, what would you like to do differently?

_____

The Talking Stick and Answering Feather

Objective

To develop skills in culturally sensitive practice with Native people

_____

_____

This exercise can be conducted as a class activity or in groups of five to twenty people. For this exercise you will need symbolic objects to represent your talking stick and answering feather. The talking stick has been used for many centuries by Native American tribal peoples as a means of controlling just and impartial communication. The person in the group who is holding the talking stick has the right to talk. It is said that the person who holds the stick in his or her hands holds the sacred power of words (Herring, 1999). When he or she is finished speaking, the stick is passed to whomever wishes to take it next. If the person desires an answer to a question from someone, he or she can pass the answering feather to that person.

Instructions are available at various Web sites on how to make a talking stick using symbolic elements. See http://www.makingfriends.com/na/na_talking_stick.htm.

In class, use the talking stick format to facilitate group discussion of your feelings, opinions, and perspectives on teenage pregnancy. If you have already addressed this material, you can use the format to discuss any relevant topic.

When this method is used with clients, it is advised to have the group members participate in making the talking stick and answering feather together. Activities such as this can build cohesion and help the group form a unique identity. Once the symbolic objects have been made, the group then "owns" something. Their use can be revisited at each group session. This empowering exercise is appropriate for older children, adolescents, and adults.

Chapter 18
Groups with Immigrants

Purpose

Perhaps now more than during any other period of history, social work and other helping professions have an ethical imperative to serve immigrant populations. In the United States and in other Western countries, there is a growing anti-immigrant sentiment, which has coincided with an increase in the criminalization of undocumented immigrants (Furman, Ackerman, Loya, Jones, & Negi, 2012). This antipathy also coincides with the increasing influence of globalization on all aspects of human existence. The interconnectedness of global markets, the ability of people around the world to connect over the Internet, and other factors have led to a rise in transnational forces affecting people's daily lives (Negi & Furman, 2010). That is, people are becoming less and less dependent on borders at the same time that some politicians and groups wish to make borders more secure. This conflict has created escalating hardships for immigrants throughout the world and has increased the need for a variety of services.

Many immigrants to the United States come from communities characterized by collectivist values, and as such, groups are a natural part of their lives. Additionally, many undocumented immigrants experience a great deal of social isolation; groups can be used to help connect them with others in similar situations, helping them feel less isolated and connecting them with practical resources and opportunities (Akinsulure-Smith, 2012).

An anti-oppressive perspective (see chapter 13) is essential for working with immigrants. Perhaps more than with any other population, it is essential that a nuanced analysis of environmental and contextual factors should inform the provision of services to immigrants. Breton (1999) explores the value of a structural approach, which highlights the importance of "looking at the opportunities or barriers to full economic, social, political and cultural participation of immigrants and refugees in their new society" (p. 11). Even groups that are slightly more micro or problem specific must consider the overall aims of social justice and the social barriers to full participation that immigrants often experience. Failing to pay close attention to the sociopolitical contexts of immigration will harm a worker's ability to be fully empathic with immigrants and will reduce the relevance of the services provided.

Structure

There are several important considerations when beginning a group with immigrant populations. First, systematic barriers that many, if not all, immigrants experience can lead to a profound sense of distrust. Agencies that wish to start groups for immigrants, and who do not have experience with a particular immigrant community, should collaborate with other community groups and social service agencies that have credibility within the community. It is also important to have bilingual and bicultural group leaders; if the agency is unable to find such professionals, the leader of a group may wish to seek a co-leader from the community. Chen, Budianto, and Wong (2010) explore this balance in their examination of a group for undocumented immigrant students: "Once this support group is formed, the counselor needs to strike a balance between imparting information and exploring individual concerns, and between recognizing the grim reality for undocumented students and instilling hope for the future" (p. 359).

In their discussion of the development of groups for immigrant parents, Gonzalez, Lord, Rex-Kiss, and Francois (2011) note a similar balance when they discuss their theoretical foundation, which is "based on the premise that if immigrant parents are given the opportunities to develop relationships, social networks, mutual aid, and a sense of self-efficacy and self-awareness, they will feel empowered and will become more adept at caring for themselves and their families" (p. 24).

While anti-oppressive groups commonly note that there are often incidental individual benefits to social change and empowerment, groups for immigrants would be well served to consciously and explicitly work toward individual, group, and social aims.

Role of Leaders

When working with immigrants, the leader should adopt a role as a knowledgeable expert, yet remain a facilitator rather than an authoritarian. This apparent paradox is often difficult for some social workers to understand, but in fact such a role is congruent with the values of many immigrant populations in the United States, especially Latinos. Latinos and many other immigrant communities highly value professional knowledge. Early on in his career, the first author worked in an agency serving Latino immigrants. Many of the clients referred to him as "doctor," in spite of his not having a doctorate at the time. This *respeto* (respect for authority) is important, but workers should be comfortable about presenting their expertise and knowledge in a way that does not diminish group members. At the same time, the role of the group leader should be to facilitate interaction, mutual aid, and group decision making. They can and should give their opinions, especially when asked, but only after members of the group have spoken, and only as one voice within the group.

Role of Members

As mentioned, one of the key aims in working with immigrants is to help them achieve full empowerment and participation in the group. As groups are micro-cosms for society, the goal should be to help members move from group-level to community-level empowerment. While the same may be true for other populations, group member participation in the planning and implementation of the group holds special importance when working with immigrants. Additionally, in order to facilitate social inclusion and decrease isolation, group members can be encouraged to exchange telephone numbers and social networking information among themselves and to develop close and personal relationships with other members of the group (Delgado & Humm-Delgado, 1982). Although this goes against traditional U.S. notions of "boundaries," it should be noted that these notions are based more upon white, middle-class values than the needs of many immigrant populations (Watts-Jones, 2010). Helping group members develop relationships with each other can facilitate the inclusion of their values in the group experience and expand the group's capacity for community building (Gutierrez & Ortega, 1991).

Exercises

Uncovering Your Beliefs

Objective

To identify potential biases that may interfere with practice

---

Regardless of where you practice, chances are you will encounter undocumented immigrants. In fact, there are currently nearly 10 million undocumented immigrants living within the United States. Many people have internalized a good deal of what society tells us about various undocumented immigrants. For example, some people erroneously believe that undocumented immigrants commit a disproportionate number of violent and sexual crimes, even though research shows just the opposite is true (Ackerman & Furman, 2013). For ten minutes, write down your feelings about undocumented immigrants. Do not hold back, and do not censor yourself. After you have finished, put what you wrote away for several days, then come back to what you wrote and answer the following questions.

Writing and Reflection

1. Which of your beliefs could interfere with your practice with undocumented immigrants?

---

2. Which, if any, of your beliefs may conflict with the values of the profession?

_____

3. If you identify any beliefs that may not be congruent with social work or other human services disciplines, what can you do to bring them into alignment?

_____

4. Are there any beliefs that you hold that you might be willing to change if you had more information? If so, do some research and see if you can modify your beliefs.

_____

Understanding the Trauma of Immigrants

Objective

To gain an appreciation of the traumas that many immigrants face

_____

_____

Ask group members to brainstorm and list on a large piece of paper all of the difficulties that immigrants face. Ask them not only to speak from their experience but also to list the difficulties faced by other immigrants they know. After this exercise, divide into pairs and rank the experiences from most to least traumatic. Come back together into the larger group and discuss your rankings and the factors that you considered for ordering them as you did.

During the exercise, whether done as part of an in-class exercise or in a group with immigrants, group leaders should stress the need for psychological safety. In their introduction to the exercise, group leaders should assure members that they need not participate if doing so is too painful. Of course, should a group member begin to feel intense emotions, the exercise can be stopped and the person can be given the space to discuss his or her experiences, if he or she wishes. Group leaders must always remember that people are far more important than exercises.

Designing Groups for Immigrants

Objective

To develop skills in designing groups for immigrants

_____

_____

Using what you have learned in this chapter, along with the skills you have learned thus far in your studies generally, design a group for immigrants in your community. If you do not understand the needs of immigrants in your community, do some research prior to working on this assignment. Make sure to review chapter 2 on planning a group before you write your group plan. Consider what issues will be special for immigrants in general, and for those in your community in particular.

More Intensive Option for Students

Work in teams to develop a five-page grant application for a new group work program within an agency. Sections of this grant application should include a description of the population and the problems they encounter, the nature of the proposed services, a budget, and how the services will be evaluated. This exercise is particularly valuable for courses in program administration or macro practice.

Chapter 19
Group Work with Latinos

To understand group work with Latinos, one must understand a bit about the population in general. Latinos are an extremely diverse population; treating them as a single homogeneous group is not without its pitfalls (Furman, Langer, Sanchez, & Negi, 2007). Most Latinos speak Spanish; however, some speak Portuguese or Native languages. Most are Catholics, yet a growing number are evangelical Christians, and some are even Jewish. However, Latinos do share many common historical and cultural similarities and often share common value systems that differ from those of other ethnic groups in America (Furman & Negi, 2007). This introduction will focus on how these values affect group work practice.

When engaging in any social work practice with Latinos, it is essential that one have an understanding of their cultural values. While a full discussion of these values is beyond the scope of this chapter, we will explore a few here. First, Latinos value collectivism more than individuality. In other words, Latinos are naturally more comfortable within group contexts, provided other conditions, which we shall discuss, are met. For Latinos, family goals often supersede personal goals. This can be frustrating for non-Latino practitioners, who can view Latinos' allegiance to the family as a lack of boundaries, problems with individuation, or self-abuse. Fortunately, group leaders can utilize this norm to help establish group cohesion. Second, Latinos value *personalismo*, close personal relationships. Latinos often find the dominant American culture cold and impersonal. It is especially important to be warm, empathic, and personal. In work with Latinos, providing information about your own family and some personal history can be a valuable means of establishing a sense of trust. In groups, this translates to allowing enough time for group members to get to know each other. Third, family is extremely important to Latinos. At times, group leaders working with Latinos may feel that group members are getting off topic when members are talking about problems and concerns with family and friends. This is a part of the culture; family comes first, often even before oneself. Therefore, sometimes Latinos need the opportunity to vent about family issues before they can focus on presenting problems not related to family issues and concerns. Fourth, respect is very important in Latino communities. This is especially true in group situations. Latinos may interpret being confronted or challenged as disrespectful. It is therefore important that group leaders establish a quality helping relationship and help members understand their methods before any directive confrontation is used.

When one is working with Latinos in groups, it is important to understand each group member's cultural and historical background. Assuming that someone came to this country from elsewhere can be dangerous. Latinos have been living in the western part of the United States for over 150 years! Making assumptions about language skills, country of origin, and even identification as a Latino can hurt a group worker's credibility. It is important for group workers to be open and learn about group members' cultural experiences and realities.

Vasquez and Han (1995) found that standard group practices are based upon Eurocentric values and must be adapted to Latinos. Notions of independence, self-sufficiency, and autonomy are largely individualistic conceptualizations. As previously mentioned, Latinos often place their own needs and interests after those of their families. It is important that group leaders do not misinterpret expressions of this cultural norm as being indicative of poor boundaries or low self-esteem.

Group leaders must also view time differently when working with Latinos. Latinos view time as being less important than relationships and other values. As such, lateness to a group does not necessarily signify that the group is not important; time is just viewed in less absolute terms—disrespect is not intended. It is often valuable to have the first portion of a group structured in such a way that it can be more fluid and less formal (e.g., the use of dyads or triads, or a warm-up activity).

Díaz et al. (2007) assert that Latino values must be infused not only into each group session, but into the very structure and nature of the group. This means that *personalismo,* the importance of the family, respect for Latino culture, and the importance of language must be considered in the promotion, organization, formation, planning, work, and evaluation of the group (Vasquez & Han, 1995).

An important consideration when one is forming a group is the stigma that Latinos feel regarding therapy and helping. *Machismo*, or the ascribed cultural rules regarding men's behavior, makes some Latino men less likely to admit to problems or seek help. Both men and women worry that admitting needing professional help means admitting that they are crazy. Others worry that seeking help in a small, tight-knit community will bring scorn or shame to the family. As such, confidentiality is an extremely important value that must be discussed repeatedly in the group process.

Regardless of the type of direct practice group that is formed, it should have a strong mutual aid component. Due to the collectivist nature of Latino groups, the mutual aid model of group work is suggested. Group members should be encouraged to share their personal experiences and examples of how they have resolved complex psychosocial problems that are often experienced differently by different ethnic groups. The skills and facilitation discussed previously in this book will be invaluable. However, Latinos have a great respect for authority and knowledge. As such, workers are encouraged to provide direct feedback and advice when they are asked. Providing concrete information on how to solve problems leads group members to respect the leader. This balance of empowering group members but being willing to be direct is often difficult for group workers to attain and demands practice and a great deal of self-reflection and planning.

While the focus of this chapter is on work with Latinos, much of it applies to culturally sensitive practice in other populations. By exploring your own strengths and limitations, reactions and biases, you will begin to develop the awareness you need for working with Latinos and other cultural and ethnic populations.

Exercises
Community Interview

Objectives

- To develop interviewing skills
- To develop knowledge about Latino culture and cross-cultural commoditization skills
- To practice task group skills

In-Class Exercise

In task groups of four, you will work to develop a list of interview questions that will guide your interview with a member of the Latino community. Your questions should be designed to help you understand the cultural experience of Latinos. You should develop a plan for where and how you will access members of the community. Then, using the interview questions that you developed, interview a member of the Latino community.

Writing and Reflection

1. Describe what it was like conducting your interview.

_____

2. What parts of the interview were most difficult for you?

_____

3. What do you believe you did well?

_____

4. What would you like to have done differently?

_____

5. What did you learn that will help you in your group work practice?

_____

Exploring Differences and Commonalities

Objectives

- To increase your ability to see people holistically
- To develop your ability to place cultural influences within the context of individual differences and universal commonalities

Furman (2002) developed a model for understanding the individual based upon social constructionism. Social constructionism allows for the integration of three crucial domains of human consciousness and behavior: that which pertains to the individual, that which pertains to all people, and that which pertains to specific groups and cultures. Figure 2 is a graphic representation of this perspective. For example, one might know that in traditional Guatemalan culture, birth control is typically perceived as being against the will of God. Conscious attempts at limiting family size are seen as meddling with the divine. A practitioner only looking at culture would assume that this culturally ascribed belief would cause a client to be highly resistant to birth control measures.

Figure 2   Social Constructionism

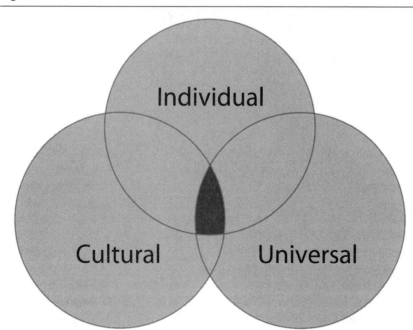

However, the social constructionist would suggest that cultural manifestations exist only in how they are interpreted by the individual. For instance, a particular woman might view this socio-religious doctrine as applying only to abortion and not to contraception. She may feel the weight of the values and norms that she learned from her socio-religious context but may make an individual decision to act differently based upon her own personal free will.

In-Class Exercise

Take turns leading small groups of five to eight in class. For ten minutes, lead a discussion of one of the topics listed below, or choose your own topic.

- Discipline of children
- Disagreeing with one's parents
- The roles of men and women in performing housework
- Parents living with their adult children
- The importance of education for education's sake (not merely to obtain a career)
- Abortion (Be careful with this controversial topic.)

If the topics are controversial, the leaders will want to make clear to the group that the purpose of their discussion is to understand each other's perspectives, not to agree or disagree. The leader will want to facilitate a discussion about how individuals have developed their beliefs, including information from each of the three domains discussed above.

Discussion in Dyads

With a partner, conduct a multicultural assessment of your partner in regard to the topic you discussed. For ten minutes, see if you can determine the distinct role that each domain has played in shaping his or her beliefs and behavior. Many find it useful to draw the three domains as they are depicted in figure 2 and place information in each circle. You may find that many beliefs, emotions, and behaviors fall in more than one domain, thus illustrating the dynamic interaction of human behavior and learning.

Writing and Reflection

1. What did you learn from this exercise?

_____

2. How might what you learned be useful in assessment?

_____

3. How might what you learned be useful in group work?

_____

Group Design Exercise

Objective

To learn to apply the skills of planning to group practice with Latinos

In-Class Exercise

In this exercise, you will work in small groups. Imagine that you have been given responsibility for several groups to serve the needs of your community's Latino population. Your agency, a small community-based program, provides mental health and family supports to mostly Central American immigrants. Your agency director has become concerned that the specific needs of Latinos have not been addressed. She has given social workers the task of developing groups to address the following concerns: immigration issues, employment issues, the use of culturally appropriate helpers, and domestic violence.

In groups of four, you will create groups to address each of these concerns. For each concern, you will want to address the following issues.

1. What type of group would be most appropriate?

2. How will you recruit clients for this group?

3. What are some potential topics to be discussed?

4. What are some interventions that you may use?

5. What culturally specific factors will you need to address?

6. What are some of the potential pitfalls of creating such a group?

7. What types of agency supports will you need?

8. How will you evaluate the group?

Latino Case Example

Objective

To develop an understanding of group work with Latinos

Case Example

The following case is based upon a group at a Latino-serving agency in a city in the northeastern United States. The majority of the clients in this agency are Puerto Rican, yet the agency serves a sizable percentage of African American clients and other Latinos as well. In this case, we will explore the group from the perspective of a specific individual, to help you develop an appreciation of the lived experience of a group member.

Martha Torres is a twenty-eight-year-old Puerto Rican woman who was born on "the Island" (what Puerto Ricans often call their homeland). Martha has been attending the agency's substance abuse program for the last four months. Martha was arrested for selling marijuana and was mandated to attend treatment for her alcohol, marijuana, and cocaine use. Martha's probation officer has also asked Martha to get career counseling. Martha actually has a college degree from a good university. Martha received her degree in sociology and originally wanted to be a college professor. However, Martha decided to live on the mainland United States for several months after her graduation in Puerto Rico. While there, she fell in love with an older man who she now says was *muy malo* (very bad). Only after she fell in love did she realize that he was a drug dealer and a pimp. Martha tried to break up with the man but found herself returning to him. She was in love, and she oddly felt taken care of by him. Besides, she was also afraid of him and his subtle and sometimes not so subtle threats of violence. Instead of returning home, she lived with him and began to use drugs. This started a several-year spiral into addiction and prostitution. After three years, Martha returned home and continued to engage in her addiction and prostitution to support her habit. Martha then returned to the mainland and was arrested for selling cocaine shortly after.

Since it was Martha's first offense, she was able to enter a community corrections program and was placed on parole with mandatory treatment. During Martha's several months in the program, she did not attend group. Her probation officer did not mandate that she attend group sessions. However, after a relapse, which she admitted to her counselor, she agreed to attend group therapy. Martha was scared at first. She is a very proud woman (*orgullosa*) and did not want to shame her family by admitting her feelings to strangers. This was especially true since members of the group had distant yet real family and kinship connections—not uncommon within the Puerto Rican community in this city. However, at the first session, the group worker reinforced confidentiality and cautioned against *chisme* (gossip).

Over time, Martha found herself enjoying group. She found she often heard her own story in the stories of others. She related to people's struggles and stories of triumph. In group, she heard practical advice about a variety of issues. She also found that her story could be of help to others. One of the women in her group struggled with ending a relationship that was similar to the one that started Martha on the road into addiction. Martha told her story and stressed how she wished she had found a way to break free sooner. She said that she was saddened that she wasted so many years with this man, and in her addiction. While telling her story, Martha began to cry. The woman to whom she was telling her story got up and gave Martha a hug. Martha found herself letting go and broke down in tears. Now no longer self-medicating her feelings with drugs, Martha began to experience a profound sense of grief and loss. She began to wail loudly, a culturally accepted means of expressing these feelings. After she stopped crying, Martha apologized for her emotional outburst. The group members, calling her "sister," told her that they were grateful to her. The woman who hugged Martha thanked her for the gift of her story. The group worker reinforced the value and power of Martha's catharsis and also validated the group members for their outstanding support.

This event marked an important turning point for Martha. She slowly began the process of rebuilding her life. She soon found a job as a barista in a coffeehouse and began taking classes at the local community college. Martha frequently has to resist the temptation to use drugs but uses her supports well. For the first time in years, she feels a sense of hope and pride. She plans to return to Puerto Rico after she attends school for nursing, and for the first time in years she hopes to find a man to love and marry.

Writing and Reflection

1. What other services may be of value to Martha?

2. What cultural factors influenced her treatment?

3. If you were conducting a group such as this, what theories would you incorporate?

Chapter 20
Group Work with People with HIV/AIDS

Although the rate of AIDS mortalities in the United States is declining, new HIV infections continue to occur and create life challenges for those infected with and affected by the virus. The face of AIDS is changing. In earlier days of the pandemic in the United States, the virus was linked to the gay population, primarily white males engaging in sex with other men. Currently, epidemiological data show that African American women who contract HIV through heterosexual relationships are the largest source of new infections. As the face of people living with AIDS changes, so do our social work interventions need to adapt to the change.

Group interventions for HIV-positive people and HIV-affected people (family, friends, and caregivers of people who are infected) occur in a variety of settings. They are most commonly held in AIDS service organizations, connected to infectious disease units in hospital settings, sponsored by county health departments, or operated through churches or other religious-based groups. Because of the way that HIV/AIDS affects an individual's health, it is uniquely important for the group leader to coordinate with medical professionals, nurses, nutritionists, and others in order to track group participants' health challenges. In most cases, group involvement should augment, not replace, other medically based services. It is recommended that group leaders have a general medical knowledge of the HIV/AIDS disease progression and understand how it relates to the psychosocial dimensions of the condition, although it is not necessary to be an expert (Smith & Curell, 1998).

A diagnosis of HIV carries with it an array of psychosocial concerns. Stigma around disclosure is common, and it is not unusual for individuals to lose their social support networks. From an empowerment perspective, because isolation and loneliness are common psychosocial outcomes for people living with HIV/AIDS, group work is generally a favorable option (Mancoske & Smith, 2004).

Although groups can be effective with all subgroups of people living with HIV/AIDS, there are a few populations that are especially suited for group work. Adolescents who are infected or affected have positive group experiences due to their tendency to turn to peers for guidance at this developmental stage (Mancoske & Smith, 2004). Gay men also do well in homogeneous groups because they may have family-of-origin networks and social support networks that are characterized by rigidity or hostility. Positive relationships built in group settings can become a type of "family of choice" and reduce feelings of estrangement or isolation (Mancoske & Smith, 2004). Furthermore, groups have been shown to provide benefits including symptom decrease, improved quality of life, reduced emotional distress, and a sense of finding meaning in life (Mancoske & Smith, 2004). Leserman, Petitto, Golden, Gaynes, Gu, Perkins, et al. (2000) reported that stress and denial speed up the progression of HIV, and evidence-based practice certainly indicates that support group interventions are essential components of HIV/AIDS care.

Social workers interested in doing group work with people living with HIV or AIDS must decide at the outset what kind of group it will be. The group may be open ended or time limited; it may be psychoeducational or based on mutual aid (i.e., a support group). When one is choosing a location for the group meetings, extra care must be paid to accessibility. There is an axiom in the field of AIDS work that says, "If you aren't poor when you are infected with HIV, you will become poor because of it." Since the axiom often proves itself true, groups should be held at locations close to public transportation. Due to the physically debilitating effects of the disease, easy handicapped and wheelchair access is a necessity (Smith & Curell, 1998). Aronstein (1998) identified some specific accommodations for HIV-infected clients. He recommends using overstuffed chairs and keeping the group meeting room well heated, since being cold or uncomfortable can be a barrier to success. Due to a phenomenon called wasting, people with AIDS are often struggling to keep weight on, and this may cause them to feel cold and be uncomfortable sitting on chairs without padding. Perhaps the most important feature of the location of the group is that provisions should be made for maximizing privacy (Smith & Curell, 1998). Group members may experience anxiety at the prospect of being recognized by others in the area, thus having their HIV-positive status revealed without their consent.

Group composition for people with or affected by HIV/AIDS can vary depending on need. Infected and affected people can be mixed, as they can provide support to each other, or they can be separated into more homogeneous groups, with a more specific focus on relevant issues. Groups for recently assimilated Latinos with AIDS are commonly held in Spanish, and culture-specific groups also exist for African American males and females. One recommendation is that groups not be segregated based on method of transmission of the virus. Efforts should be made to minimize stigma around the method of infection. Regarding stage of illness, those who are newly diagnosed with HIV can meet separately from those with a diagnosis of AIDS. However, it is also helpful to conduct mixed groups so that the newly diagnosed can learn important skills such as antiretroviral medication adherence from those who have been living with the virus for many years.

Group leaders working with people living with HIV/AIDS must be aware that group members may be subject to revolving-door hospitalizations and even to death. Groups focusing on HIV/AIDS typically enjoy a high level of cohesion due to the fact that many of the issues discussed there are not addressed elsewhere in the members' social networks. Therefore, when members become ill, are hospitalized, or die, the group will likely have a strong reaction. Sometimes the death of a group member draws the group together and opens the door for deeper discussion of members' fears and sadness about their own situations. Group leaders should be prepared for these events and help the group normalize their grief reactions.

Exercises
Exploring Our Biases

Objective

To explore biases and prejudices that may affect your work with those who are culturally different

---

Most of us, whether we admit it or not, have internalized prejudiced beliefs. It is nearly impossible to have grown up in a society that is inundated with sexism, racism, classism, anti-Semitism, and homophobia and not have been influenced by these ideologies and beliefs. Exploring our biases and prejudices is one of the most painful things we can do, but one of the most liberating as well. When we recognize the influence of these often subtle beliefs, we can work to ensure they do not affect our group leadership. To deny possessing these thoughts gives them power over our leadership style by robbing us of our most important tool, our self-awareness.

Writing and Reflection

Since these are often difficult issues to address, complete these questions in a place where you feel safe. If you do not wish to keep the answers in this workbook, you may write them on a separate piece of paper and, if you wish, destroy it when you are done.

1. Think of the different ethnic groups in your community. What have you come to believe about them that may not be true?

---

2. Do you have any thoughts or beliefs about certain ethnic or cultural groups in your community that automatically come to mind when you are in their presence?

---

3. Are you uncomfortable around certain groups of people? What feelings do you have around them?

_____

4. How is your behavior different when you are around members of different ethnic or cultural groups?

_____

5. Do you have any beliefs about men or women that may be overly generalized or untrue?

_____

6. Are you comfortable around people who are gay, bisexual, or transgender? What beliefs do you have about people who are members of these groups?

_____

7. Are there any groups with whom you may be uncomfortable working? How might this affect your social work practice?

_____

Empathic Understanding of Losses

Objective

To develop empathy for difference

In-Class Exercise

Conduct this exercise in small groups in class. This activity can also be done in a therapeutic group, to teach empathy. Pass out five index cards to each person. Instruct everyone to write on each card one of the top five things they value in their lives. Examples could be their relationship with their spouse or parents, their home, going skiing, their faith and church involvement, their pet, spring break vacations, spending time with friends, taking care of their car, or watching their children grow up. There will likely be a wide variety of responses. Next, each person holds the cards up to the person on his or her left and asks that person to pick a card. The group is then told to imagine that this element in their life is gone (e.g., they no longer have their home, a particular relationship, or the ability to go skiing). They are told to examine what it would feel like to experience this loss. Then, they are asked to turn to the person on their right and ask that person to pick a card. They then internalize this subsequent loss. Draw an analogy to what it is like to be diagnosed as HIV positive or as having AIDS. With these determinations come losses of jobs, homes, friends, relationships with family, abilities to do activities, health, financial security, and often plans for the future. This activity is also appropriate for developing empathic understanding of what it is like to be elderly, placed in an assisted living facility or a nursing home, or seriously disabled.

Writing and Reflection

1. What did you write on your five index cards?

2. What cards were taken from you?

3. How did you feel when these cards were taken from you?

4. How would your life be different if you truly did lose these two elements of your life?

Class Discussion

1. This chapter advises against categorizing HIV/AIDS group members according to their method of transmission (e.g., intravenous drug use, sex between two men, sex between a monogamous heterosexual couple, mother-to-child transmission). Why do you think this advice was offered? Do you agree? What would be the consequences of separating clients in this manner?

2. This chapter mentions that the face of AIDS has been changing from primarily a disease of gay white men to one that affects heterosexuals as well, particularly African American women. How might this shift in the client population manifest in group membership? How might a group leader need to adapt to this shift?

Understanding Our Cultural Identity

Objective

To develop an increased sense of your own cultural identity

By learning to understand their own cultural identity, social workers develop a sense of how cultural factors affect our behavior. This is especially important for group leaders, who often lead groups with members of various cultural groups.

Writing and Reflection

The questions below are meant to be written exercises. They may also be discussed in dyads, in small groups, or with the entire class.

1. Describe your cultural and ethnic origin and identification.

   _____

2. In what ways is your culture important to you?

   _____

3. What are the key values of your culture? How might these values differ from the values of other cultures?

   _____

4. How might these differences in values lead to conflicts with others?

   _____

5. How does your cultural background influence your behavior in groups?

   _____

6. Describe a time when you have felt different, or like an outsider. What was it like? How was your behavior different in this situation than in other situations?

   _____

7. How does your gender affect your behavior in groups? How does it affect your behavior toward those of the same and different genders?

   _____

8. What religious or spiritual issues affect your behavior in groups?

   _____

Discuss a few ways that you can become more in touch with your cultural background.

Epilogue

What Did You Learn?

As you worked your way through this book, you engaged in a variety of exercises that we hope have increased your repertoire of practice skills. To begin our epilogue, we would like you to do one more exercise to help you explore and concretize what you have learned.

1. What were the most important lessons you learned from reading the chapters?

   _____

2. What skills did you learn as a result of working through the exercises in the book?

   _____

3. What do you feel are your current strengths as a group worker?

   _____

4. What skills do you wish to improve?

   _____

5. What is your own personal philosophy of group work?

   _____

6. Based upon your answers, develop a plan for your own professional growth and development.

   _____

Your ability to understand your own strengths and weaknesses, and how these may affect your ability to lead various types of groups, is an essential skill of group practice. Your answers to the preceding questions, and indeed your answers throughout the workbook, can be viewed as the beginnings of a self-assessment that can guide your professional growth. It is essential that you engage in personal and professional growth experiences throughout your career. Helpers often believe that receiving their MSW marks the end of their professional education, when, in fact, it marks the very beginning. The first author often asks students what kind of social worker does not need supervision. The response, said with tongue planted firmly in cheek, is "A dead one." Throughout our careers, we are challenged by new clients, new situations, and changes in our own personal lives. We grow, and we change. We find certain situations push our buttons, and we must learn how to respond. Social work practice is constantly changing and evolving; we also need to change and evolve as well. We hope you come to view the process of self-reflection and the development of self-awareness as essential aspects of your practice.

The Future of Group Work

At this point, we would like to discuss a few changes in society that we believe will have a profound effect on how group work will be provided in the future, and the profession's response to those changes. While the exact nature of social transformations is often hard to predict, what is clear is that the rate of social change has been accelerating and will continue to do so (Kreuger, 1997; Postman, 1992).

An Increasingly Diverse Society

While American society has always been diverse, this diversity is expected to increase. Immigration, birthrate disparities, and the integration of the world's economies will continue to make America an increasingly diverse country. Latinos are currently the largest ethnic minority in the United States, constituting 17 percent of the population. By the year 2025, Latinos are expected to make up nearly 25 percent of the population (Furman & Negi, 2007). Not only are Latinos moving to areas with traditionally large Latino communities, but they can now be found in urban, rural, and suburban areas that have had historically low percentages of Mexicans and Central and South Americans. As such, all social workers must become prepared to provide culturally competent services to these and other diverse communities. Developing the ability to speak Spanish not only is a good practice skill but will ensure your employability!

Throughout the United States, the demographics of numerous ethnic communities are changing. Social workers must learn to understand the role that groups can play in helping these communities and their members achieve their goals and dreams. Social workers will have to decide whether to create and run groups specifically designed for these ethnic communities (homogeneous groups), cross-cultural groups (heterogeneous groups), or a combination of the two. Further research is needed to ascertain when and how these groups can be formed and can function.

Globalization and Hypertechnologies

Two of the biggest changes that social work must contend with are globalization and the development of new forms of technology that change the very fabric of society. While scholars in social work have begun to think about the impact of globalization on society, actual changes in practice models have not followed. Group workers will need to develop methods that account for the shifting and changing nature of a world that is made smaller by the integration of national economies and the advent of advanced computer-based technologies.

While the vast majority of group work should take place in person, new technologies allow for new possibilities for providing services to difficult-to-serve populations. Furman, Negi, Schatz, and Jones (2008) explore the possibility of using Internet and telephonic technologies to coordinate services for transmigrant populations. Through the visual and audio conferencing functions of

Skype or other Internet communication systems, service providers working in multiple countries can coordinate services for families whose lives span two or more nations. Imagine being able to have a treatment planning group for a substance-abusing client in New York who frequently travels between the United States and his home country of Guatemala. Including his wife and minister in Guatemala may allow the client to experience a level of support that would not be possible without the use of technology-assisted group work.

The Future of Group Work as a Method

As we mentioned in chapter 1, the prominence of group work as a method has diminished over the last several decades. This is unfortunate, as group work is an approach that is so congruent with social work values. In the future, social workers would be wise to recommit to group work practice. This is particularly true for workers who use approaches that transcend the micro/macro divide. This recommitment is akin to going "back to the future." Social workers have a rich legacy from which to draw. We hope that you take the opportunity to explore the rich history of group work practice. While it is important always to seek new innovations, there is no reason to reinvent the wheel.

It is our hope that over the next few decades social workers will rediscover and develop group work in several areas. First, the humanities and the arts, including poetry, have been shown to have some strong potential uses with many populations (Collins, Furman, & Langer, 2006). Using the arts in group practice is congruent with the strengths-based approach that lies at the core of social work values. Second, groups are an ideal means of providing a bridge between macro and micro practice. Groups that help empower people to make changes in their communities can also be a valuable means of helping people increase their sense of self-efficacy and self-esteem. Third, in the age of managed care and diminishing financial resources for services, social workers will need to increasingly evaluate their practice. The ability to demonstrate the efficacy of group work will help ensure its survival. Fourth, social workers must recommit to developing educational and training programs that specifically focus on group practice. We hope that you have come to appreciate and enjoy being a group worker. Wonderful changes can happen for clients within groups—we hope you are able to witness and be part of many such events in your careers!

References

Ackerman, A., & Furman, R. (2013). The criminalization of immigration and the privatization of the immigration detention: Implications for justice. *Contemporary Justice Review, 16*(2), 251–263.

Adolescent Pregnancy Prevention Coalition of North Carolina (2004). *Recipes for success: Fresh ideas for teen parent programs*. Durham, NC: Author.

Akinsulure-Smith, A. M. (2012). Using group work to rebuild family and community ties among displaced African men. *Journal of Specialists in Group Work, 37*(2), 95–112.

Anderson, J. (1997). *Social work with groups: A process model*. Boston: Allyn & Bacon.

Anderson, J., & Brown, R. (1980). Life history grid for adolescents. *Social Work, 25,* 321–322.

Andrews, J. (2001). Group work's place in social work: A historical analysis. *Journal of Sociology and Social Welfare, 24*(3), 211–235.

Anorexia Nervosa and Related Eating Disorders (2005). *Treatment and recovery.* Retrieved March 15, 2008, from http://www.anred.com/tx.html

Aronstein, D. (1998). Organizing support groups for people affected by HIV. In D. M. Aronstein & B. T. Thompson (Eds.), *HIV and social work: A practitioner's guide* (pp. 242–258). New York: Harrington Press.

Association for the Advancement of Social Work with Groups (2010). *Standards for social work practice with groups* (2nd ed.). Alexandria, VA: Author.

Austin, M. J., Coombs, M., & Barr, B. (2005). Community-centered clinical practice: Is the integration of micro and macro social work practice possible? *Journal of Community Practice, 13*(4), 9–30.

Bank, A. L., Arguelles, S., Rubert, M., Eisdorfer, C., & Czaja, S. J. (2006). The value of telephone support groups among ethnically diverse caregivers of persons with dementia. *The Gerontologist, 46*(1), 134–138.

Barry, T. D., Klinger, L. G., Lee, J. M., Palardy, N., Gilmore, T., & Bodin, S. D. (2003). Examining the effectiveness of an outpatient clinic-based social skills group for high-functioning children with autism. *Journal of Autism and Developmental Disorders, 33*(6), 685–701.

Bensussen-Walls, W., & Saewyc, E. M. (2001). Teen-focused care versus adult-focused care for the high-risk pregnant adolescent: An outcomes evaluation. *Public Health Nursing, 18*(6), 424–435.

Birchall, H. (1999). Interpersonal psychotherapy in the treatment of eating disorders. *European Eating Disorders Review, 7,* 315–320.

Boal, A. (1993). *Theatre of the oppressed*. New York: Theatre Communications Group.

Boyer, D., & Fine, D. (1992). Sexual abuse as a factor in adolescent pregnancy and child maltreatment. *Family Planning Perspectives, 24*(1), 4–11.

Brandler, S., & Roman, C. P. (1999). *Group work: Skills and strategies for effective interventions* (2nd ed.). New York: Haworth Press.

Breton, M. (1999). The relevance of the structural approach to group work with immigrant and refugee women. *Social Work with Groups, 22*(2/3), 11–29.

Brigman, G., & Campbell, C. (2003). Helping students improve academic achievement and school success behavior. *Professional School Counseling, 7*, 91–98.

Brown, N. W. (1998). *Psychoeducational groups.* Philadelphia: Accelerated Development.

Brown, R. (1988) *Group processes: Dynamics within and between groups*. Oxford: Blackwell.

Burlingame, G. M., MacKenzie, K. R., & Strauss, B. (2004). Small group treatment: Evidence for effectiveness and mechanisms of change. In M. J. Lambert (Ed.), *Handbook of psychotherapy and behavior change* (5th ed., pp. 647–698). New York: Wiley & Sons.

Cassidy, K. (2007). Tuckman revisited: Proposing a new model of group development for practitioners. *Journal of Experiential Education, 29*(3), 413–417.

Chen, E. C., Budianto, L., & Wong, K. (2010). Professional school counselors as social justice advocates for undocumented immigrant students in group work. *Journal for Specialists in Group Work, 35*(3), 355–361.

Collins, K., Furman, R., & Langer, C. L. (2006). Poetry therapy and cognitive therapy. *The Arts in Psychotherapy, 33*, 180–187.

Dass, R., & Gorman, P. (1985). *How can I help?* New York: Alfred A. Knopf.

Delgado, M., & Humm-Delgado, D. (1982). Natural support systems: Source of strength in Hispanic communities. *Social Work, 27*(1), 83–89.

Dennis, B. (2009). Acting up: Theater of the Oppressed as critical ethnography. *International Journal of Qualitative Methods, 8*(2), 65–96.

DeRoos, Y. S. (1990). The development of practice wisdom through human problem-solving processes. *Social Service Review, 64*, 276–287.

DeRosier, M. E. (2004). Building relationships and combating bullying: Effectiveness of a school-based social skills group intervention. *Journal of Clinical Child and Adolescent Psychology, 33*(1), 196–201.

Devan, S. G. (2001). Culture and the practice of group psychotherapy in Singapore. *International Journal of Group Psychotherapy, 51*(4), 571–577.

Díaz, M. L., Fuenmayor, M. J., & Piedrahita, S. (2007). *En español: Group psychotherapy with Latino/a clients.* Paper presented at the annual convention of the American Group Psychotherapy Association, Austin, TX.

Doel, M. (2006). *Using groupwork.* New York: Routledge.

Dominelli, L. (2002). *Anti-oppressive social work theory and practice.* New York: Palgrave Macmillan.

Douglas, S., & Machin, T. (2004). A model for setting up interdisciplinary collaborative working in groups: Lessons from an experience of action learning. *Journal of Psychiatric and Mental Health Nursing, 11,* 189–193.

Ephross, P. H. (2005). Social work with groups: Practice principles. In G. L. Greif & P. H. Ephross (Eds.), *Group work with populations at risk* (2nd ed., pp. 1–14). New York: Oxford University Press.

Fernandez, L. M. (1997). Running an effective task group: The five C's. *The New Social Worker Online Magazine, 4*(1), 1–3.

Franklin, C., Corcoran, J., & Harris, M. B. (2004). Risk, protective factors and effective interventions for adolescent pregnancy. In M. W. Fraser (Ed.), *Risk and resiliency in childhood and adolescence* (2nd ed., pp. 75–87). Washington, DC: NASW Press.

Freire, P. (1970). *Pedagogy of the oppressed.* New York: Continuum.

Freire, P. (1993). *Pedagogy of the oppressed.* New York: Continuum.

Furman, R. (2002). *Culturally sensitive social work practice with Latinos.* Doctoral dissertation. Yeshiva University, New York.

Furman, R. (2007). Faculty self-reflection and study abroad: An expressive approach to autoethnography. *Reflections, 13*(4), 18–30.

Furman, R., Ackerman, A., Loya, M., Jones, S., & Negi, N. (2012). The criminalization of immigration: Value conflicts for the social work profession. *Journal of Sociology & Social Welfare, 39*(1), 169–185.

Furman, R., Langer, C. L., & Anderson, D. K. (2006). The poet/practitioner: A new paradigm for the profession. *Journal of Sociology and Social Welfare, 33*(3), 29–50.

Furman, R., Langer, C. L., Sanchez, T. W., & Negi, N. J. (2007). A qualitative study of immigration policy and practice dilemmas for social work students. *Journal of Social Work Education, 43*(1), 133–146.

Furman, R., & Negi, N. J. (2007). Social work practice with transnational Latino populations. *International Social Work, 50*(1), 107–112.

Furman, R., Negi, N. J., Schatz, M. C. S., & Jones, S. (2008). Transnational social work: Using a wrap-around model. *Global Networks: A Journal of Transnational Affairs, 8*(4), 496–503.

Furr, S. (2000). Structuring the group experience: A format for designing psychoeducational groups. *Journal for Specialists in Group Work, 25*, 29–49.

Garcia, M. S. (2004). Effectiveness of cognitive-behavioral group therapy in patients with anxiety disorders. *Psychology in Spain, 8*(1), 89–97.

Garvin, C. (1997). *Contemporary group work* (3rd ed.). Boston: Allyn & Bacon.

Garvin, C. (2005). Group work with seriously mentally ill people. In G. L. Greif & P. H. Ephross (Eds.), *Group work with populations at risk* (2nd ed., pp. 31–45). New York: Oxford University Press.

Garvin, C., & Tropman, J. (1998). *Social work in contemporary society* (2nd ed.). Boston: Allyn & Bacon.

Gerhart, U. C. (1990). *Caring for the chronically mentally ill.* Itasca, IL: Peacock.

Gitterman, A. (2006). Building mutual support in groups. *Social Work with Groups, 28*(3/4), 91–106.

Gitterman, A., & Shulman, L. (Eds.). (2005). *Mutual aid groups, vulnerable populations, and the life cycle* (3rd ed.). New York: Columbia University Press.

Glassman, Y., & Kates, L. (1990). *Group work: A humanistic approach.* Newbury Park, CA: Sage.

Gonzalez, A., Lord, G., Rex-Kiss, B., & Francois, J. J. (2011). Patients beyond borders: A social group work curriculum for supporting immigrant parents and building solidarity. *Social Work with Groups, 35*(1), 18–34.

Gutierrez, M. L., & Ortega, R. (1991). Developing methods to empower Latinos: The importance of groups. *Social Work with Groups, 14*(2), 23–43.

Hall, A. (1985). Group psychotherapy for anorexia nervosa. In D. Garner & P. Garfinkel (Eds.), *Anorexia and bulimia* (pp. 213–239). New York: Guilford Press.

Haney, C., & Zimbardo, P. (1998). The past and future of U.S. prison policy: Twenty-five years after the Stanford Prison Experiment. *American Psychologist, 53*(7), 709–727.

Hays, D. G., Arredondo, P., Gladding, S. T., & Toporek, R. L. (2010). Integrating social justice in group work: The next decade. *Journal for Specialists in Group Work, 35*(2), 177–206.

Hendrickson, E. L., Schmal, M. S., & Ekleberry, S. C. (2004). *Treating co-occurring disorders: A handbook for mental health and substance abuse professionals.* Binghamton, NY: Haworth Press.

Herring, R. D. (1999). *Counseling with Native American Indians and Alaska Natives: Strategies for helping professionals.* Thousand Oaks, CA: Sage.

Hill, C., & Thompson, B. (2003). Therapist use of silence in therapy: A survey. *Journal of Clinical Psychology, 59*(4), 513–524.

Hirokawa, R. Y., Degooyer, D., & Valde, K. (2000). Using narratives to study task group effectiveness. *Small Group Research, 31*(5), 573–591.

Howlin, P., & Yates, P. (1999). The potential effectiveness of social skills groups for adults with autism. *Autism, 3*(3), 299–307.

Humphreys, K. (1999). Professional interventions that facilitate 12-step self-help group involvement. *Alcohol Research and Health, 23*(2), 93–98.

Jackson, R. L. (2001). *The clubhouse model: Empowering applications of theory to generalist practice.* Belmont, CA: Brooks/Cole.

Jacobs, E. E., Masson, R. L., & Harvill, R. L. (2001). *Group counseling: Strategies and skills.* Pacific Grove, CA: Brooks/Cole.

Johnson, D. W., & Johnson, R. T. (1996). Conflict resolution and peer mediation programs in elementary and secondary schools: A review of the research. *Review of Educational Research, 66*(4), 459–506.

Johnson, D. W., & Johnson, R. T. (2005). *Teaching students to be peacemakers* (4th ed.). Edina, MN: Interaction Book Company.

Koch, M. O., Dotson, V. I., & Troast, T. P. (1997). Interventions with eating disorders. In C. Zastrow (Ed.), *Social work groups: Using the class as a group leadership laboratory* (pp. 242–268). Chicago: Nelson-Hall.

Kreuger, L. W. (1997). The end of social work. *Journal of Social Work Education, 33*(1), 19–27.

Kurland, R. (1978). Planning: The neglected component of group development. *Social Work with Groups, 1*(2), 173–178.

Kurland, R., & Salmon, R. (1998). *Teaching a methods course in social work with groups.* Alexandria, VA: Council on Social Work Education.

Ladouceur, R., Sylvain, C., Boutin, C., Lachance, S., Doucet, C., & Leblond, J. (2003). Group therapy for pathological gamblers: A cognitive approach. *Behavior Research and Therapy, 41*(1), 587–596.

Lane, P. S. (1995). *Conflict resolution for kids: A group facilitator's guide.* Washington, DC: Taylor & Francis.

Lane-Garon, P. (2000). Practicing peace: The impact of a school-based conflict resolution program on elementary students. *Peace & Change, 25*(4), 467–482.

Lane-Garon, P., McWhirter, J. J., & Nelson, E. (1997). *Building a peaceful community: A handbook for implementing a school-based conflict resolution program.* Tempe: Arizona Information Systems.

Leserman, J., Petitto, J. M., Golden, R. N., Gaynes, B. N., Gu, H., Perkins, D. O., et al. (2000). Impact of stressful life events, depression, social support, coping, and cortisol on progression to AIDS. *American Journal of Psychiatry, 157*, 1221–1228.

Lewin, K. (1951) *Field theory in social science: Selected theoretical papers.* New York: Harper & Row.

Lindsey, L. L. (2010). *Gender roles: A sociological perspective* (5th ed.). Boston, MA: Pearson.

Lucas, J. W. (1999). Behavioral and emotional outcomes of leadership in task groups. *Social Forces, 78*(2), 747–776.

Mancoske, R. J., & Smith, J. D. (2004). A generalist practice model in HIV/AIDS services: An empowerment perspective. In R. J. Mancoske & J. D. Smith (Eds.), *Practice issues in HIV/AIDS services* (pp. 60–80). New York: Haworth Press.

Martin, J. A., Hamilton, B. E., Sutton, P. D., Ventura, S. J., Menacker, F., & Kirmeyer, S. (2006). Births—final data for 2003. *National vital statistics reports, 54*. Hyattsville, MD: National Center for Health Statistics.

Mcintosh, P. (1990). White privilege: Unpacking the invisible knapsack. *Independent School, 49*(2), 31–36.

Miller, D. L. (2003). The stages of group development. A retrospective study of dynamic team processes. *Canadian Journal of Administrative Sciences, 20*(2), 121–134.

Mueser, K. T., Bolton, E., Carty, P. C., Bradley, M. J., Ahlgren, K. F., DiStaso, D. R., et al. (2007). The trauma recovery group: A cognitive-behavioral program for post-traumatic stress disorder in persons with severe mental illness. *Community Mental Health Journal, 43*(3), 281–304.

National Association of Social Workers (2000). *Code of ethics of the National Association of Social Workers.* Washington, DC: Author.

Negi, N., & Furman, R. (2010). *Transnational social work practice.* New York: Columbia University Press.

Niemann, S. H. (2002). Guidance/psychoeducational groups. In D. Capuzzi & D. R. Gross (Eds.), *Introduction to group counseling* (3rd ed., pp. 84–101). Denver, CO: Love.

Northen, H., & Kurland, R. (2001). *Social work with groups* (3rd ed.). New York: Columbia University Press.

Organista, K. (2000). Latinos. In J. R. White & A. S. Freeman (Eds.), *Cognitive-behavioral group therapy: For specific problems and populations* (pp. 281–303). Washington, DC: American Psychological Association.

Postman, N. (1992). *Technopoly: The surrender of culture to technology.* New York: Random House.

Rapp, C. (1985). Research on the chronically mentally ill: Curriculum implications. In J. P. Bowker (Ed.), *Education for practice with the chronically mentally ill: What works?* (pp. 32–49). Washington, DC: Council on Social Work Education.

Ratts, M. J., & Santos, K. N. T. (2010). The dimensions of social justice model: Transforming traditional group work into a socially just framework. *Journal for Specialists in Group Work, 35*(2), 160–168.

Razack, N. (1999). Anti-discriminatory practice: Pedagogical struggles and challenges. *British Journal of Social Work, 29*(2), 231–250.

Ringel, S. (2003). The reflective self: A path to creativity and intuitive knowledge in social work practice education. *Journal of Teaching in Social Work, 23*(3/4), 15–28.

Roffman, R. (2004). Psychoeducational groups. In C. D. Garvin, L. M. Gutierrez, & M. J. Galinsky (Eds.), *Handbook of social work with groups* (pp. 204–222). New York: Guilford Press.

Rosenbaum, M. (1996). *Handbook of short-term therapy groups.* New York: Jason Aronson.

Rubin, A., & Babbie, E. (2008). *Research methods for social work* (6th ed.). Belmont, CA: Wadsworth/Thompson Learning.

Sakamoto, I., & Pitner, R. O. (2005). Use of critical consciousness in anti-oppressive social work practice: Disentangling power dynamics at personal and structural levels. *British Journal of Social Work, 35*(4), 435–452.

Salmon, J., Ball, K., Hume, C., Booth, M., & Crawford, D. (2008). Outcomes of a group-randomized trial to prevent excess weight gain, reduce screen behaviors, and promote physical activity in 10-year-old children: Switch-play. *International Journal of Obesity, 32,* 601–612.

Salvendy, J. (1999). Ethnocultural considerations in group psychotherapy. *International Journal of Group Psychotherapy, 49*(4), 429–464.

Sands, R. G., & Gellis, Z. D. (2011). *Clinical social work practice in behavioral mental health: Toward evidence-based practice* (3rd ed.). Boston: Allyn & Bacon.

Santilli, N., & Hudson, L. (1992). Enhancing moral growth: Is communication the key? *Adolescence, 27,* 145–160.

Schön, D. A. (1983). *The reflective practitioner: How professionals think in action.* New York: Basic Books.

Schwartz, W. (1971). On the use of groups in social work practice. In W. Schwartz & S. Zalba (Eds.), *The practice of group work* (pp. 3–24). New York: Columbia University Press.

Shapiro, J. L., Peltz, L. S., & Bernadett-Shapiro, S. T. (1998). *Brief group treatment: Practical training for therapists and counselors.* Pacific Grove, CA: Brooks/Cole.

Sheafor, B. W., Horejsi, C. R., & Horejsi, G. A. (1994). *Techniques and guidelines for social work practice* (3rd ed.). Boston: Allyn & Bacon.

Shera, W. (Ed.). (2003). *Emerging perspectives on anti-oppressive practice.* Toronto: Canadian Scholars' Press.

Shulman, L. (2009). *The skills of helping individuals, families, groups, and communities* (6th ed.). Belmont, CA: Thompson.

Shutz, W. C. (1958). *FIRO: A three dimensional theory of interpersonal behavior.* New York: Holt, Rinehart & Winston.

Smith, M., & Curell, A. (1998). Clinical issues in groups for HIV-infected individuals. In D. M. Aronstein & B. T. Thompson (Eds.), *HIV and social work: A practitioner's guide* (pp. 78–91). New York: Harrington Press.

Soltys, F. G., Reda, S., & Letson, M. (2002). Reminiscing and the group process. *Journal of Geriatric Psychiatry, 35*(1), 50–61.

Spidel, A., Lecomte, T., & Leclerc, C. (2006). Community implementation success and challenges of a cognitive-behavior group for individuals with a first episode of psychosis. *Journal of Contemporary Psychotherapy, 36*(1), 51–58.

Steinberg, D. M. (2004). *The mutual-aid approach to working with groups: Helping people help one another* (2nd ed.). New York: Haworth Press.

Stevahn, L., Johnson, D. W., Johnson, R. T., Oberle, K., & Wahl, L. (2000). Effects of conflict resolution training integrated into a kindergarten curriculum. *Child Development, 71*(3), 772–784.

Strier, R., & Binyamin, S. (2010). Developing anti-oppressive services for the poor: A theoretical and organisational rationale. *British Journal of Social Work, 40*(2), 1908–1926.

Tadaka, E., & Kanagawa, K. (2007). Effects of reminiscence group in elderly people with Alzheimer's disease and vascular dementia in a community setting. *Geriatrics and Gerontology International, 7*(2), 167–173.

Toseland, R. W., Jones, L. V., & Gellis, Z. D. (2004). Group dynamics. In C. D. Garvin, L. M. Gutierrez, & M. J. Galinsky (Eds.), *Handbook of social work with groups* (pp. 60–72). New York: Guilford Press.

Tuckman, B. W. (1965). Developmental sequence in small groups. *Psychological Bulletin, 65*(6), 384–389.

Tuckman, B. W., & Jensen, M. A. (1977). Stages of small-group development for practitioners. *Journal of Experiential Education, 29*(3), 413–417.

Ulman, R. B., & Abse, D. W. (1983). The group psychology of mass madness: Jonestown. *Political Psychology, 4*(4), 637–661.

Vasquez, M. J. T., & Han, A. L. (1995). Group interventions and treatment with ethnic minorities. In J. F. Aponte, R. Y. Rivers, & J. Wohl (Eds.), *Psychological intervention and cultural diversity* (pp. 109–127). Boston: Allyn & Bacon.

Washington, O. G. M., & Moxley, D. P. (2003). Group interventions with low-income African American women recovering from chemical dependency. *Health and Social Work, 28*(2), 146–156.

Watts-Jones, T. (2010). Location of self: Opening the door to dialogue on intersectionality in the therapy process. *Family Process, 49*(3), 405–420.

Weinberg, H. (2003). The culture of the group and groups from different cultures. *Group Analysis, 36*(2), 253–268.

Westwood, M. J., Mak, A., Barker, M., & Ishiyama, F. I. (2000). Group procedures and applications for developing sociocultural competencies among immigrants. *International Journal for the Advancement of Counselling, 22*(4), 317–330.

Williams, R., & Williams, V. (1994). *Anger kills: Seventeen strategies for controlling the hostility that can harm your health.* New York: Harper Perennial.

Wing Lo, T. (2005). Task-centered groupwork: Reflections on practice. *International Social Work, 48*(4), 455–465.

Yalom, I. D. (2005). *The theory and practice of group psychotherapy* (5th ed.). New York: Basic Books.

Zastrow, C. (2005). *Social work groups: Using the class as a group leadership laboratory* (5th ed.). Chicago: Nelson-Hall.

Index

About the Authors

Rich Furman, MSW, PhD, is professor of social work at the University of Washington, Tacoma. Professor Furman is the author of *Practical Tips for Publishing Scholarly Articles: Writing and Publishing in the Helping Professions,* and co-author of *Navigating Human Service Organizations.* His over one hundred books, articles, and chapters focus on social work practice with transnational Latino populations and the role of the arts and humanities in social work practice, education, and research. Professor Furman teaches direct practice courses, with a special focus on group work. He has many years of experience engaging in clinical, macro, and educational groups.

Kimberly Bender, MSW, PhD, is associate professor at the University of Denver Graduate School of Social Work, where she studies methods for improving services and developing empirically based interventions for adolescents at risk of problem behavior. Through ongoing projects researching youth with co-occurring disorders, runaway/homeless youths, and maltreated adolescents, she has published numerous peer-reviewed journal articles. Professor Bender has worked in a variety of clinical settings providing group treatment to youths, including residential treatment, inpatient units, and outpatient mental health centers.

Diana Rowan, PhD, MSW, LCSW, is currently an assistant professor at the University of North Carolina at Charlotte. She earned her PhD in social work from the University of Texas at Arlington, and her MSW from Our Lady of the Lake University of San Antonio. She has fifteen years of clinical social work practice experience and has conducted group work in chemical dependency, inpatient psychiatric, correctional, and private practice settings, and with specific populations such as people living with HIV/AIDS and people with chronic mental illness.